LEFT-HANDED SCISSORS

LEFT-HANDED SCISSORS

ANGELA BELLI-INFANTE

Text Maegan Clearwood, on behalf of Story Terrace

Design Adeline Media, London

First print August 2018

www.StoryTerrace.com

DEDICATION

To my husband, Massimo, who was not only my biggest fan, but also my biggest supporter, best friend, and someone who loves my scars: thank you for accepting me just the way I am. I love you. To my mother who was my advocate and personal comedian: you got me to laugh when I wanted to cry. Thank you for your constant perseverance in fighting for my accomodations. You were the best nurse ever. To my Great Uncle James V. Polio, for believing in me when I was growing up and having faith in my abilities to do anything able-bodied people could do. To my cousin, Nicholas P. Ferrucci, whom I am so happy to have in my life. To my Godchild Sophia Colonna: I hope you find something from this book. You mean the world to me. To my nieces, Gabriella Rose and Sara Ann: you were like my own, and even when you gave me a hard time at the Discovery Store or Build-A-Bear, I hope I have touched your life the way my Great Uncle affected my life. I hope I have inspired you to dream big. I am only a text away if you ever need anything, but I hope you know I would rather chat in person or over lunch. Don't ever forget me. To my sisters Maria and Carla, thank you for always helping me. I love you both and appreciate all of the moral support and physical help you have given me throughout the years. You are not only my sisters, you are my best friends. I want to thank all of my caretakers, nurses, physical therapists, occupational therapists, medical doctors, counselors, physical education teachers, grade school teachers, my prosthetist, and all of the professionals who have assisted me throughout my life. Thank you to my personal trainers at DAC and my coaches at Tony Robbins; thank you for lighting the fire in and under me – lol. To my brothers-in-law, my entire extended family, and my dad, for such a hard work ethic. I hope you realize that you were the steady foundation in my life. Thanks for always providing food and shelter. I love you, you big teddy bear!

CONTENTS

FOREWORD

Angela is an amazing young woman who has inspired and enlightened me in life, and I trust that, through this book, she will inspire others. In this book, she tells how she has continued to learn, persevere, laugh, meditate, focus, and hold a smile in her heart regardless of pain or illness. She has life experience that makes her uniquely qualified to engage and enlighten others when their bodies "don't cooperate" with their plans, dreams, and goals. She illustrates how she gives her illness only the attention it requires and uses most of her energy instead to grow and thrive as a joyful, strong, dynamic, aware, and caring person. Her story is engaging and it generates hope. I also wanted to say that the book is an easy read and very good. I think it is a great entry to working with kids with health challenges. I think that her sharing her story will encourage others who are presented with health challenges at various stages of their lives, as well as offer direction to those who care for, work with, or love people who are dealing with health issues. It is a book worth reading.

Maggie Goodwin LCSW

1

THE HAND

"Tiny and Fragile"

It was a cold winter day in March, perfectly normal for New England weather. The radiator heat was roaring and the neighbors were over. Mom was preparing dinner and waiting for Dad to pull up in his dump truck after another long, back-breaking day. My sister Carla and I were playing baseball in the yard. Everything was perfectly typical until I collapsed from a pain in my left knee.

You would never have believed it, but I was a lemon – not the fruit, but the car. I looked strong on the outside, but my childhood was a series of illnesses and emergencies and pain. In fact, if I were to print out my full medical history, page for page, I could probably fill an entire hospital wing at the old Fitkin Five children's unit at Yale. But before the illnesses struck, I was an unremarkably normal girl: two arms, two legs, no tumors. Perfectly average.

Before I fell ill for the first time, my childhood was relatively uneventful. I was raised in the city, West Haven, Connecticut, in a tiny home of 900 square feet that housed three girls in one room and my parents in the other. It was tight: we had extended family living upstairs, along with the occasional renter. The house was constantly abuzz with company and coffee, round the clock. We were cramped and rarely with money to spare, but we were happy.

For the first few years of my life, I took many of my favorite pastimes for granted – climbing on Dad's truck and waving at the passersby, running, playing double dutch, tumbling around outside. Little did I know that soon, the activities that so many children enjoy without thought or care would become mountainous challenges. While my peers played catch and tag, just learning to write would soon become a struggle for me.

It was during one of these silly outdoor excursions that my world suddenly fell to pieces. My sister Carla, 11 at the time, noticed that I wasn't talking. We were playing baseball with some neighborhood friends in our small concrete backyard (laid beautifully by my father, a bricklayer, but it could be better described as a sterile driveway than a yard) when I collapsed on our cellar door. A child complaining of a painful knee would usually elicit nothing more than a "quit whining" from most parents, but something in my eyes must have tipped my sister and my mother off to something more serious. As a teenager, I would complain about my mother's overprotective, even coddling nature, but that afternoon, her keen instincts saved my life.

I was rushed to my primary care doctor, who scoffed at my mother, dismissing her as a nervous Nellie and advising us to go home. My parents were told, however, to keep an eye on me and to seek further help if I started developing spots on my skin. That very night, I had a rash. Later, I projectile vomited specks of blood, an indicator of internal bleeding. I had a fever of 105 degrees. And, signaling further trouble, the rash erupted into black and blue marks all over my body.

My parents rushed me to the ER, where a closer examination confirmed my mother's instincts that something was truly wrong. As I was wrenched from my father's protective arms, the physicians somberly informed my parents that I might not survive the night. I was already in shock at that point, slipping in and out of consciousness, and I was put into an induced coma to keep me stable. I spent 55 days in the hospital, 13 of which were in that coma.

I remember fleeting moments from that first day: a needle looming over me, a nurse telling me to bite the pillow as they gave me gigantic syringes full of medicine in my thighs. I recall the oxygen tank I was trapped inside, the procedure they had to prepare in order to cut down on my wrist after my veins collapsed, my mother screaming in the hallway as the doctors strapped me down to a steel bed. I remember rolling my eyes as nurses tried to trick me into eating giant horse pills folded into vanilla ice cream, my Aunt Patty whispering prayers in my ears and bringing me homemade apple sauce, and Grandma's grilled cheese sandwiches. I will never forget my cousin

Donna's gift of candy in a brown paper bag, all the colors and flavors of different confections to wash down my yucky medicine, including the disgusting yellow pill for my heart. I even remember being in the coma, my family surrounding me in what I thought was a dream. I vaguely recall seeing a semi-circle of people around me asking me to wake up. My family filled my room with love; their prayers were like a phone calling me to come back and be with them again.

I couldn't pronounce my diagnosis, let alone understand it: bacterial meningitis, or meningococcemia. They have vaccines to prevent it now, but as a kid growing up in the '70s, I was an open target. My immune system was down and I had probably been around a person or animal that was carrying the disease. The disease quickly turned into an infection. I remember doctors trying to save my right hand, picking and prodding at my arm, trying to find healthy cells from the gangrene. Ultimately, my wrist had to go to prevent the infection from traveling to my brain. But they managed to save my elbow, which was a huge benefit for me.

I still have medical reports from that first hospital stay – at least six inches of pages worth – which state, in beautiful, calligraphy handwriting, my progress from day to day:

Angela is a four-and-a-half year old who presented 18 days ago with fulminant meningococcemia. Predicted mortality was 90%. She came to the floor five days ago and has the following problems: 1) necrotic right hand and forearm, 2) there are also neurotic post purpomic lesions on the extremities and back,

3) swollen tender left knee, 4) Left foot cellulation. Dr Allen is meeting with family to discuss various issues including the AMPUTATION. He will be very helpful with Brenda Smith in working with family. They are also (Ms. Smith) working on the financial aspects: NO INSURANCE.

I was to find out later that my parents had, just a few weeks before my illness struck, terminated insurance with a company and were waiting the necessary three months before switching to a new one. My near-death experience had struck at the worst possible time for my parents. According to a newspaper article about my illness, the initial hospital bill was more than $25,000 – not including doctor's fees, additional surgery, physical therapy, or my prosthesis.

Luckily, word spread quickly about my condition. Neighbors and friends and even strangers gathered funds for my hospital bills. Soon, there were enormous garbage bags delivered to my hospital room, overflowing with donated toys and stuffed animals.

Despite all the goodwill and yummy treats, the fact remained: my hand was going to be amputated. My parents struggled to find a way to tell me this monumental news. Someone at the hospital even gave me a handmade book to help me understand what was going to happen, in which I was introduced to Debbie, who "had been very sick."

Her blood had an infection. The doctors and nurses gave her medicine to help her body get better. Soon she was feeling much, much better. All except her hand. It stayed sick. The doctors wrapped it in bandages because it was black and hard and it didn't work anymore. After awhile the doctors said it was time for Debbie to have an operation to take away the part of Debbie's hand that was still sick and hard and black. How do you think Debbie felt?

The book was filled with simple drawings of Debbie: sitting with her mommy and daddy as the doctor tells her the news, lying on the operating table and in her wooden hospital bed, and finally going home with her new prosthesis. By the end of the story, aside from her new hook, Debbie looks perfectly normal, getting dressed by herself and playing with her sisters. "What other things can you think of that Debbie could do?" the book asked.

When the big day of surgery arrived, I planned ahead by preparing a milkshake to enjoy post-op. Even at four years old, I could sense the uneasiness in the room as my mother wrung her hands in worry and the nurse bustled about, adjusting and preparing various implements. I did my best to lighten the mood the only way I knew how: by spilling some of my milkshake as a distraction. Unfortunately, this only increased the tension, as the nurse barked at me for being clumsy. I responded in kind by running around the room in my Wonder Woman underoos and repeating a word I'd heard Carla scream at Maria – behaviors that didn't exactly make anyone feel better.

Despite this chaotic pre-op, my surgery went as smoothly as could be expected. I consulted my Debbie book for guidance after surgery, and it remains in my scrapbook to this day. Alongside it is a card filled with bubbly cursive and words of encouragement from my newfound hero, Carol Johnston. Carol had been born without her right arm, which didn't stop her from becoming an award-winning gymnast. She sent me a letter, which I read in my hospital bed: "I really don't think having one arm is a handicap," she wrote. "In fact, I consider myself very lucky... Just work hard, get well, and keep smiling."

Like Debbie and Carol, I would work hard, and I got mostly well soon enough. But of course, it would be a long time until I felt normal again, and a good many years before I felt as strong and capable as the likes of a professional gymnast.

There's a picture of me in that newspaper feature. I'm in a frilly, floral dress, short enough to show off the bandages on my knee and right hand. Behind me, a painting of Jesus is taped to my hospital room wall (my mother's doing I have no doubt). The caption reads, "ANGELA BELLI: Tiny and fragile, but alive."

I'd never thought of myself as tiny, certainly not fragile. I was the tomboy of my family, always ready to help my father out with his household projects and the first to run errands for the family. My mother had always been on the protective side, certainly, but I'd never felt coddled or smothered or breakable. Little did I know that this hospital visit marked the beginning of the rest of my childhood: one of constant hospital visits – and one with a mother who never wanted her daughter in danger again, even if it meant keeping her at home.

Coming Home

Up until eighth grade, I would spend my days in and out of school, as well as in and out of a prosthetic. In fact, I can determine how old I am in class photographs, not based on my hairstyle or clothing, but by my prosthesis (or lack thereof): in my first grade photo I have a forced smirk on my face, my sleeve covering where my right hand used to be. The next year, I'm grinning in the front row, my new hook sitting in my lap. After that, the romance of having a prosthesis wore off, and the reality of being the Weird Kid sank in, so photos show me sans hook more often than not.

I never felt more like an outsider than when I was sick enough that I had to be homeschooled, which happened far more often than I would have liked. My mother couldn't drive at that point, so it was cheaper (taxis were expensive), easier, and, in her eyes, safer to just keep me home. In many ways, I don't take after my mother: I never mastered her skills in the kitchen, nor did I mesh with her traditional notions of what it meant to be a good little Italian lady. While my friends spent their mornings at school and afternoons around the neighborhood getting scraped knees and chasing each other, my mother preferred that I stay safe and sound indoors.

For all the times I rolled my eyes because my mother acted like I was made of glass, I also couldn't deny that she was one of my closest companions. She made my hospital visits bearable, never leaving my bedside and surprising me every morning through a peephole square window just the size of her tiny head. I would wait in anticipation for her arrival like clockwork. At 7 a.m., Mom would pop her head in the big hospital wooden door. Dad must have gotten the McDonald's orange juice before going to work and dropping Mom off at the hospital because Mom was always there to make sure I ate my hospital scrambled eggs and ketchup (Mom put the ketchup on so I would eat the eggs). For lunch, mostly on the weekends when Dad was home, she would surprise me with McDonald's cheeseburgers she made my dad get at the restaurant. My favorite of her tricks was when she made fun of all the screeching babies in the children's ward. She silently opened and closed her mouth to the tune of their wails so that she looked like a giant ventriloquist baby. She always made me laugh when I had to get shots. She would even make monkey faces by pulling her ears out and having her tongue slide under the top of her lip, moaning like a monkey to keep me entertained.

Mom was a masterful parent. She had the monumental job of taming my two older sisters in public, and somehow always managed to do so with dignity and grace. She even knew how to conquer thunderstorms; whenever winds and cracks of thunder rattled our windows, Mom would let us camp out on the bathroom floor and eat junk food until the rain passed. And when we weren't scared, Mom had an arsenal of clever tricks to play on us. Right around bedtime, after the lights were out, she would don a veil and chase my sisters around the house. I was too scared to play along, so I followed behind her, holding tightly to the backs of her knees and begging her to take mercy on Maria and Carla.

Life with my family was both a safe haven and a world of chaos; crazy beautiful is what I remember. I shared one small room with my older sisters, Maria and I sharing the same bed. My sisters fought – constantly and viciously – so little me was often stuck in the middle, trying to temper their uncontrollable spats. "Stay out of my stuff!" Carla would screech from one corner of the room, drowning her hair in Aqua Net as she prepped for another date. Carla had enough hairspray to open a small salon, and no matter how often we washed the floor, her daily spritzes would soon recoat the linoleum so that it felt like we were walking on a layer of sticky notes.

The rest of our house was no quieter. The upstairs was constantly occupied, first by renters who never paid my parents and eventually threw a refrigerator down the front stairs. There was also my Aunt Marie with my cousin Paulie. Then there was Zia Elaine and Zio Ennio (for years I didn't realize that *zio* meant *uncle* in Italian, so I called him "Zio Uncle Ennio" – when my father finally corrected me, I was mortified) and cousins Sergio and Loredana; we were their first home after they emigrated from Italy. My father's parents even lived with us for a while before returning to Italy, although I don't remember that chapter of our house's history. Meanwhile, amidst all the hustle and bustle typical of an overflowing Italian family, my mother ran the financial side of my father's bricklaying business, so when she wasn't cooking or cleaning, she was tied to the telephone (my sisters and I would later discover the party line).

Luckily, I had my secret hideaways to escape from the madness. The first was the closet in the entry hallway, where I stowed my favorite stuffed animals and toys; I even slept there if my bedroom was too loud. My other hiding place was the basement. Navigating my way downstairs was always terrifying because the upstairs light only stretched five feet before I was met by a stretch of total darkness; I had to feel my way to the dangling light switch at the end of the hallway. Beyond that spine-tingling entrance, however, the basement was peaceful, serene, and all mine. We had a stereo system that stretched nearly the length of an entire wall – perfect for listening to my favorite vinyl records or the radio – and I had my state-of-the-art boombox when I wanted to play my cassettes. This was the ultimate space to play with my Cabbage Patch Kids (genuine and knock-off) or write on my chalkboard and play teacher. If I was very careful, I could prop open a latch on the basement window, sneak out, and bike to 7/11 for some candy. The basement was even air conditioned, but not for my or any other human's comfort.

The precious cargo that was actually being kept cool was my father's famous homemade wine. He stored his beloved concoctions downstairs so that the smell of fermenting grapes constantly permeated the air. I remember lining up to help him unload crates of grapes from the driveway. Then, my sisters and I were recruited to join in the smashing process.

My father had a vat that crushed the grapes, and if we helped with the crank, Maria and I would walk in a circle with the crank to crush the grapes. When we helped, we were allowed to taste the first (pre-fermented) sample of juice. He spent hours upon hours in the basement doing "quality control" before somewhat unsteadily making his way back upstairs for one of Mom's enormous Italian suppers.

Even more sacred to my father than his homemade wine, however, was The Mother – the same active culture that my great-great-grandparents had used and passed down for future generations. The Mother is a mysterious lump of what looks like a small piece of liver that floats around in wine until it turns into vinegar. My father's red wine vinegar is utterly unique, a taste that always transports me back to memories around our crowded kitchen table.

Aside from wine and vinegar and pasta sauce, our house was nearly always filled with the scent of two things: coffee and minestrone. Dad was never far from a mug of cappuccino, and Mom kept a pot of American brewing day and night. As for Mom's famous minestrone, it was always overflowing with fresh vegetables from our garden – including the dreaded beans. I was a picky eater and despised those strange, lumpy legumes with every fiber of my being. I remember trying to refuse them once, but Dad's scolding – "You're gonna eat every last one of those beans in your dish!" – scared me into swallowing them whole. I still remember the slow, painful journey they made down my throat. My strategy thereon out was to mash them up until my soup was a creamy, digestible mess.

Not only did our vegetables come straight from the backyard, but our meat did as well. We raised chickens, pigeons, rabbits, quail, even roosters from time to time. When I was younger, I relished in feeding my beloved pets, who dined like kings and queens on hand picked worms and fresh corn. When I was slammed with the truth – that my animals were not running away in the middle of the night but being slaughtered for our meals – I abstained from eating chicken, a fasting that I continued from the age of eight to 23.

Regardless of my protestations, there was no denying that the food on our table was heavenly: all fresh, organic, and with an irresistible zest of Italian flair. Mother's cooking made us neighborhood celebrities; I constantly had friends begging to play at my house because they knew she would whip up something divine while they were over. The best meals of all, however, were prepared during the holidays. In classic Italian style, each Christmas Eve was celebrated with the Feast of the Seven Fishes: a traditional, elaborate meal comprised of dish after dish of seafood delicacies. Thanksgiving was another major event, I was even given leave from my months-long hospital stay to enjoy the holiday with my entire family. I still remember the drive home, and my Grandma Rose was there. I am pretty sure I cried when my mom and dad brought me back to the hospital.

However, holidays were notable for more than the unparalleled food; they were also the rare moments when our entire, sprawling Italian family gathered to celebrate together in a few cramped rooms. Besides my parents and sisters, there was Grandmother Rose (my mom's mother), who never had a mean thing to say about anybody and whom I loved dearly, my mother's brother Uncle Ralph, the Navy veteran (thank you for serving) who helped me catch my first fish, and my Aunt Patty, the artist of the family who was constantly thinking up beautiful new creations for us to admire.

Then there was Aunt Marie, my mother's other sister. Aunt Marie, my godmother, was my mom's partner in crime, always bustling around the kitchen, gossiping, and speaking her mind. She was a waitress, and everyone knew her in town. People would confuse her face for my mom's all the time, to the point where my mom was regularly mistaken for her sister when we went out to eat. "No, I'm Anna, the other one," she'd inform the staff when they offered her a glass of wine (Mom never drank, at least not during the day). More than anything, Aunt Marie was known for her opinions. She always had something to correct me on: "You put milk in my coffee instead of half-and-half!" or "You're too young for that dress, pick something else." Aunt Marie was also the first to break the news to me that I had inherited the "Italian Curse": a thin wisp of hair above my upper lip. "We need to get rid of that," she told 13-year-old me. "Come on. We need some Jolen to bleach that away." I miss you, Aunt Marie.

Also dear to my heart were my beloved Uncle Jimmy, Aunt Ann, Aunt Eleanor, and Uncle Anthony, aunt Eleanor's husband. Uncle Jimmy was soft-spoken, meticulous, and generous; he brought a quiet, much-needed balance to our family of brassy matriarchs. He worked a big job at Tweed Airport in New Haven, but when he was with us kids, he was all silliness and smiles. He always had a joke to tell or a quarter to pull out from behind our ears. But more importantly, Uncle Jimmy was the first adult to give me permission to dream big. Whereas the rest of my family entertained old-fashioned notions about what it meant to be disabled, Uncle Jimmy made sure I had the resources to live as fulfilling a life as possible. He was my benefactor for many years, a generosity I didn't appreciate until I was older and realized how cost-exorbitant having a disability could be. He even dedicated a plaque for me in the Sacred Heart University Library, an honor that I was determined to live up to. Uncle Jimmy didn't drive, so his rare visits to our house are some of my fondest memories.

Our house was always overflowing – with people, food, smells, noise – so when even the basement and closet were insufficient solace, I would venture outdoors.

We had to rely on the bus and our feet to navigate town when Dad wasn't home, so I was no stranger to walking. I loved exploring the neighborhood and being alone with my thoughts. My favorite companion was my Grandmother; we especially loved autumn strolls, during which we would point out colorful foliage as we traipsed along Third Avenue. When I played solo, I loved playing hopscotch and jumping rope (I tied the rope to a fence to be my other hand), swinging from trees, making mud pies, and climbing every surface I could find. Despite my mother's overprotective nature and my sisters' constant bickering, I felt relatively normal at home. After all, I could do pretty much everything the rest of my family could: I ran errands for my father, took the bus, even rode a bike. But at school, there was no denying that I was different.

I became accustomed at a very young age to ignoring crude remarks and even outright insults. I was bullied, certainly, but had plenty of tricks that helped me turn invisible. I never spoke up in class and I avoided standing out in a crowd. As much as I loved learning, I loved being normal, or at the very least not abnormal. But despite my efforts to the contrary, my frequent absences made me stick out as "the sick kid." My first months back at school, I was given a special calendar to keep track of how often I wore my prosthesis. I loved collecting the bright and colorful tokens of accomplishment, but more often than not, the chart showed that I missed school entirely.

But like my alter-ego Debbie, I still learned how to function in the world with relative ease. I was right-handed originally, so my first major task was learning how to use my non-dominant hand. I struggled with writing for years, partly because I was in and out of school so often, but also likely because of those early struggles.

Other milestones that were normal for my peers proved difficult for me. My first prosthetic was much cruder than my later models. In fourth grade, when I convinced myself that I wanted to learn to play the violin, we had to stuff my hook with clay to keep the bow in place. I also dreaded art class, where I was never able to track down the pair of dull, green-handled, left-handed scissors. I watched in envy as my friends created beautiful collages, cut out perfectly and assembled to the teachers expectations. Meanwhile I missed the teacher's instructions, neglected to have dazzling artwork, and scrambled around the classroom, digging in boxes and bins just to cut out my rough painting, wanting to tear the edges because that would be faster than cutting with shears. I hated begging the teacher for instructions a second time because I missed what she had said trying to find the clippers. I got accused of being the teacher's pet and craving attention, but nothing could be farther from the truth: it was the fault of those elusive left-handed scissors.

Somehow, all of these hiccups in my early schooling didn't hinder my love of learning. I loved challenging myself and accumulating knowledge, whatever the subject. In fact, when it came to school, there was a surprising silver lining to my early medical conditions. I was in and out of the classroom and terrified of speaking up in class, but I had one advantage that my sisters and peers did not: attention. I received constant encouragement from the nurses who checked up on my progress, not only physically, but academically as well. That sticker chart made an enormous impact on my young psyche: I was determined to attend class, even when I was too old to earn stickers and treats for attendance. I knew as early as first grade that I had something to prove.

My academic pursuits confused my family members, each of who were accomplished in their own rights but had never completed high school. My parents' traditional Italian philosophy was simple: women were made to keep house and make babies, and men were meant to earn money and eat their wives' food. I was an anomaly in my disdain for cooking and staying cooped up indoors, but even more so for my ability to do virtually anything that an able-bodied person could. My mother and father were convinced that my future was going to be reliant on collecting social security checks, and that my only hope was marrying a man who was able to look past my supposed deformity. To them, the ideas of me driving, graduating, and getting a job were utter fantasies.

My grandmother saw past these superficial doubts. "You'll never have to worry about Angela," she predicted. And in most ways, she was right. I learned to be even more independent than my able-bodied sisters, to everyone's surprise. On the whole, my childhood was as normal as it could have been – for a little while, at least.

*Cousin Donna on the left and my oldest sister, Carla,
on the right, playing dolls on the famous cellar doors
that I became ill on.*

442060

MILES
TO
NORTH POLE

New Haven/Milford Mall Santa Claus

*Last photos of me with my hand playing tea with my sister,
Maria, and Dad.*

Maria and I would play on my dad's beautiful concrete porch for hours. Nice brick work, Dad!

Sister Maria and one of my favorite cousins, Joe.
(Secret: they are all my favorite!)

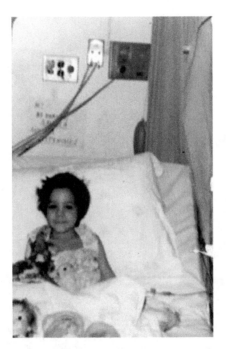

My nurse made a sign above my head that stated my name is Angela and I'm listening. I remember my mom and doctors always whispering in the hallway and I always wanting to know what they were saying about my prognosis. My mom even got me a doctors kit and these are some toys that kept me occupied for hours. Thank you to all who donated! I also gave many unused toys to the hospital and learned about donating from all the thousands of donors that gave to me.

Mom laminated the document so not to ever forget how far we have come from these somber days at the children's ward.

No doubt Mom had just changed my bandages and I am coming across some of the last photos of my hand intact.

*Maria's birthday spent in Fitkin Five recreation room. My mom always tried
to make everyone happy while celebrating Maria's birthday and having me
be within care of nurses and medical professionals. Thank you, caretakers!*

2

THE LEG

New Body, New Me

"Stop hopping around like that," my father chastised. "Quit fooling around!

"I'm not doing anything," I protested.

"You keep standing on your tiptoes. Stand up straight."

"But I *am* standing up straight."

I was 13 years old. On top of beginning to notice cute boys and other typical teenage worries, I was painfully self-conscious about my missing hand. I didn't need an additional reason to feel like the weirdo at school, but this change in my walk and new back pain – from an even-footed gait to an awkward kind of skip – was hard to ignore.

My early near-death experience should have been nothing more than a distant memory by my teen years, but lingering after effects were starting to appear. My legs were constantly sore and bruised, for instance, from knock knees, the result of early deformities from the infection. I still had spotted scars from the disease's brutal effects on my skin, and all of my teeth had been replaced after they'd turned brown from the medicine I'd been administered years ago. To complicate things more, I had resigned myself to forgoing a prosthesis altogether at this point. I was convinced that anything that was noticeably different would prompt snickering from my peers – and I had firmly decided that invisibility was superior to functionality.

So at this point in my adolescence, my father's oh-so-delicate observation of my newest complication was hardly welcome. I already felt like an outsider at school; having uneven legs was not going to help.

According to a veritable team of surgeons at Yale, there was a three-inch shortage on one side of my leg. After a second opinion from Johns Hopkins, I was left with two options: cut the the other leg, or undergo a relatively new type of leg-lengthening surgery called the Ilizarov Procedure. I opted for the latter, experimental or not. Another amputation was entirely out of the question.

At 13, I was still too young for this type of treatment. My doctors wanted to wait until I was finished growing, so I endured the awkwardness and pain of my uneven legs for another two years. To even my gait out in the meantime, I had to wear a mammoth, black shoe, earning myself the nickname Herman Munster, and I was told I need to brush my teeth. Despite my best efforts, I was now standing out in school more than ever. I resigned myself to an indeterminate period of freakishness, so instead of trying to accomplish the impossible by blending in, I embraced my boot and lack of hand. I transformed myself into what I imagined to be a female Rambo, complete with commando pants and dark, goth-inspired clothes. Despite my Girl Warrior veneer, I was embarrassed and miserable, waiting for the day when my doctors would deem me old enough for surgery.

Finally, at 15, two years after my menses started, the glorious day arrived. I wasn't destined to be very tall, my doctors said, but at least I'd be able to walk normally before long. My mother was hesitant; I imagine the trauma of seeing her youngest child come so close to death was ever-present on her mind, and the idea of subjecting me to such a painful and new type of medical treatment must have terrified her. But from my perspective, nothing was more important or worth the risk than walking with a normal shoe and being out of back pain. So I insisted on moving forward with the procedure. If all went well, I would miss a year of school but enter ninth grade looking more normal than ever.

I was to be the first person in Connecticut to undergo this type of leg-lengthening surgery. According to a newspaper article that featured this innovative procedure, this is what I went through:

The surgical procedure consists of cutting just the cortex of the bone, leaving the blood supply intact. Fine wires are passed above and below the area to be lengthened. An apparatus known as a "fixator" is fitted to the leg and allows it to be stretched ever so slowly. Angela will make the adjustment at home four times daily by turning knobs on the apparatus... Her leg will be lengthened at a rate of one millimeter a day – a slice of paper – and about an inch a month, for three months. But Angela will have to wear the apparatus for two months more for the process to be completed.

"Teen optimistic after operation," the headline reads. I'm not sure how optimistic I felt during the recovery process itself; it was incredibly painful and took a full year, after all. I was certainly optimistic going into the surgery, hoping that I would emerge a transformed, normal-looking, pain free teenager. The reality, however, involved spending months in hospital beds and wheelchairs, in and out of misery, and using special crutches; so I was probably less of a Pollyanna at the time than the reporter observed.

After my surgery, I was the designated expert on the leg-lengthening process in the state of Connecticut. As such, I was asked to talk with the second woman to receive this surgery – an interaction that introduced me for the first time to the complex and dangerous realm of addiction and pain-numbing medication.

This patient was getting not one but both of her legs lengthened, but to my amazement, seemed perfectly pain-free and positive after surgery. She beamed at me from her hospital bed: "I'm fine, it was a walk in the park!" I was embarrassed at how my post-op compared. After all, I'd had only one leg of mine lengthened, and the pain had been excruciating. Did I have a low pain tolerance? Was I overly sensitive or whiny?

Why did this woman's response seem so miraculous compared to my slow, painful baby steps toward recovery?

I inquired about this strange phenomenon with a doctor who informed me that the woman in question may have had an addiction, so of course she experienced no pain. Perhaps she was using other drugs or taking more than prescribed? "You're living life and your body was telling you when you were in pain, and that's normal," the doctor told me. "When you weren't feeling well, we knew to treat you with the appropriate drugs. It's normal to be in pain – your leg was being stretched three whole inches!"

As much as I envied the other patient's seemingly effortless road to recovery, I didn't, and still don't, regret letting pain into my world. In subsequent hospital stays, I've had ample opportunity to amp up my pain medication and completely cut myself off from discomfort. I'm keenly aware, however, of how important these painful responses are: they're my body's way of alerting me to a problem, a foreign invader was in my body and the pain was the rejection. My body was subjected to a modern day torture chamber hellish external contraption. Only in recent years have I practiced mindfulness, but the instinct to keep my body's communication pathways awake and alert has, luckily, always been present. Many times over, I faced crossroads that offered me an easy way out of my physical pain. There's another version of my life in which I not only took those paths, but became addicted to them – and for my ability to continue on the more painful but healthy path,

I am forever grateful. Plus my mom was apprehensive, and whenever I felt pain she would suggest a quarter of the pill or half. It was her hysteria that really made me appreciate the tolerance I have. I may not need narcotics, maybe I just need a tylenol or my favorite ibuprofen and ice.

Of course, at age 15, I didn't have the patience to grasp how necessary this slow journey toward physical recuperation was; I wasn't grateful so much as anxious and frustrated. I missed an entire year of school, spent nine months in a wheelchair, and was in perpetual pain – hardly the homecoming festivities that most kids my age were enjoying.

Luckily, I had a few friends who stayed by my side as I recovered. I've learned many times over since this early surgery that sickness can create unpredictable and even permanent chasms between friends. Over the years, I've lost many companions who didn't know how to react to my illnesses or placed judgment on me for my healthcare choices. This lesson – that you cannot control or fix other people, even your supposed friends – has been one of the most painful for me to learn.

My first love, in fact, drifted away because of my seemingly never-ending hospital stay. I was casually dating a boy when I was first admitted to Yale, and he astounded me by biking all the way to the hospital for a visit. "Why are you doing this?" I asked him.

"I like you!" he reassured me.

"What's wrong with you? I can't even walk!"

"You're going to be fine, and I'm going to be here for you."

Seasons changed, semesters passed, and suddenly, nine months had gone by. The sun was finally filtering in through my hospital window, and my boyfriend somberly stopped by for one last visit.

"It's springtime," he said.

"What does that mean?"

"I think I'm going to go."

It was clear to both of us that I wouldn't be joining him outdoors for summer break. I was in a walking cast at that point, so twilight walks and refreshing swims weren't in my near future. By that point, naturally, I had fallen for him, so his rejection stung, lingering long after he left my room that final time. This wasn't the last time I would place my trust in a companion, hoping they would support me for the long haul, only to be abandoned – but it was certainly one of the most painful.

Despite all the setbacks, I was determined to make the best of my leave of absence from school. This was my opportunity to start fresh, to begin high school a transformed young woman. And so, along with recuperating from my leg surgery, I decided to once and for all commit to a prosthesis, get my veneers for my teeth, and try to move on from all the losses.

I certainly wasn't being discouraged by my doctors, who told me that by avoiding the prosthesis and having an unevenness in weight, I was in danger of seriously harming my back, I already had a touch of scoliosis. I was convinced, but uneasy. Many prosthetic options at the time didn't look like they would help me fit in so much as call attention to my missing arm. Many types of hands required padding my underarms with t-shirts to avoid pain from the straps. Now that I was wearing bras and caring more about my appearance, I wanted to avoid looking lumpy and noticeably different at any cost. Ultimately, I opted for a passive hand: it would look relatively normal but wouldn't have any functionality – a perfect compromise in my eyes.

Patience wasn't in my wheelhouse at age 15, but I was forced to wait for the prosthesis to come in. Finally, I traveled to Shriners Hospital for my dainty, utterly average looking new hand– but my hopes for normalcy were shattered upon the big reveal: I had received a small man's hand. Instead of fitting in, I would stand out like a sore, plastic, oversized thumb.

I was devastated. All hopes for a high school experience free of ogling and whispers were dashed. After some heavy breathing and a few more months of waiting, however, my solution arrived: a myoelectric hand. I've since gone back to my roots and started wearing a hook again, which I've found to be the most practical option for me, but at that stage in my life, I'd finally discovered a solution that made me feel like I could finally look like everybody else and have some function.

Invisible at Last

I thrived in my newfound normalcy. My school district blended multiple junior high classes into the high school, so half of my peers had no idea who I was. No longer the Sick Girl, the Homeschooled Girl, Herman Munster, (a regular taunt before my leg surgery when I had to wear a big, black boot) or dirty teeth girl – it was as if I'd been replaced by a beautiful teenage girl who'd never missed a day of class in her life.

There were unexpected privileges to my in-recovery status as well. My leg was still fragile, so I was allowed to leave my classes early to catch the elevator to avoid crowds and pushing and shoving in the hallway, which meant time to roam the halls and hang out with my girlfriends. I was also given a pass on physical ed (PE) class for two years. Baseball was impossible, swimming and golf were difficult, ice-skating was just plain dangerous; if I wanted an activity that didn't put me at risk of landing in a cast up to my hips, I was out of luck.

My PE evasion ran out my junior year, when I was informed that I needed credits to graduate. As so often has happened in my life, a mentor and ally appeared to help me along: Ms. Poe. Instead of forcing me to participate in a conventional and potentially harmful sport, she personalized a weight-lifting class – just for me. For once, I reveled in my uniqueness. Unlike my peers, I had a space all to my own, an opportunity to build muscle and confidence and strength. I even started my own mini workout group after my girlfriends starting popping into the gym wondering why I wasn't hanging out with them in the cafe.

As an upperclassman, I gained not only strength but also independence. After years of catching the bus and walking and bumming rides from friends, I got behind the wheel and learned to drive. Driver's Ed wasn't anything special for most of my peers, but after growing up with a family convinced I would spend my life in a wheelchair, I was ecstatic.

My mother had gotten her license prior to my leg surgery so that she could make the innumerable treks to and from the hospital with ease. I took the opportunity to study alongside her, so by high school, I was a pro when it came to rules of the road. The written exam would be a breeze. But the driving test? I was terrified.

I managed to find an instructor who catered to disabled learners, and before I knew it, I had mastered the three-point turn. I was thrilled: against all odds, I was capable of conquering any milestone my able-bodied peers could manage.

High school marked a newfound confidence, something I'd never experienced before. I strutted the hallways in cool suits and dresses, partied with friends, went out with boys. In fact, when my parents announced their decision to buy a new home – a move that would throw me into an entirely different school district – I was mortified. I finally felt comfortable with my peers, and I had no desire to start all over now.

I spent less than a semester of my senior year at my new high school. I gave my parents the benefit of the doubt for that brief period of time: perhaps this new school wouldn't be as awful as I dreaded it would be. Sure enough, I excelled in my schoolwork and, for a few short weeks, it felt like things might not be a total disaster. But the very first incident of bullying – a football to the chest – was the single and final straw. I missed my old group of friends anyway, and I refused to worry myself with this new breed of insensitive bullies.

I would be returning to my old high school, no matter what. There were two things I was missing, however: an eligible address and confidence driving on the highway. Carla had moved out of the house by then, so the solution to the address obstacle was that I would live with her. The driving aspect was trickier. As adept as I was with my basic driving skills, highway driving was entirely out of my comfort zone, and I certainly couldn't get tutoring from my relatively inexperienced mother. Instead, my father helped me determine the straightest, simplest route to school, then accompanied me on my first trial drive; I remember idling on the ramp until, with a deep, wavering breath, I pressed down on the pedal, merged onto the highway, and drove faster than ever before.

I nodded at my friends my first Monday back at school as if everything was totally normal: "Told you I'd be back!" School was back in session and I felt right at home.

By my senior year, I was fit, I was confident, I was strong, and I fit right in.

One place I couldn't be invisible was in public. There's been a seismic shift in the way people treat amputees over the past decade or two – people in general are more tolerant and open-minded. But growing up was far from easy. My mother used to get furious at people who pointed and snickered:

"What are you looking at?" she'd bark at kids in the super-market.

"Ma, what are you making a big deal for?" I'd say. "They're staring because they're curious, let them look."

But kids were the least of my worries. If they were confused, they would ask questions, which I never minded. Adults, on the other hand, would ogle and whisper. "Don't stare," they'd hiss to their children, as if my missing hand were some kind of unspeakable horror or contagious.

Discrimination has manifested itself in surprising ways throughout my life. Sometimes the feeling of "otherness" has been subtle, like those instances with my mom. Other times, the discrimination has been more difficult to ignore.

Preparing for my Confirmation, for instance, put me face-to-face with this kind of treatment. I was informed that I needed to collect volunteer hours from non-profit organizations, so I began by singing to senior citizens during the holidays and being active in local pageants. I found the experience so fulfilling that I continued singing there for years after; I also collected funds for the West Haven Emergency Assistance Taskforce (our local food pantry) by going door-to-door in my neighborhood.

Unlike my girlfriends, I was completely unsure of what I wanted to do after high school – but helping people, it seemed, was my calling. And so, of my own volition, I reached out to a senior citizen home to inquire about additional volunteer opportunities. The staff seemed enthusiastic and in need of someone with my skills and passions, but oddly enough, when I arrived for the first time in person, I was informed that the position had been filled. Like many cases of discrimination, it's impossible to prove that this stemmed from the staff's belief that my disability made me unfit for the job. Something about the experience felt off to me, however, and I had the distinct feeling that it wasn't poor timing or an administrative oversight at fault, but a simple case of prejudice.

I ended up working at the dunking booth for our local carnival, so my volunteer hours were a delight to complete. This wasn't the end of my advocacy work, either, and although prejudice would factor into many milestones in my future career, it was clear that helping others was in my blood.

When it came to where these gifts and passions would take me, however, I was at a loss. All of my friends and peers had lofty plans for after graduation, but I seemed destined to stay put for the rest of my life. I'd visited my Aunt Marie's family in California some summers earlier and I fantasized about moving to the west coast for school. My parents, however, flat-out refused. No daughter of theirs was trekking across the country by herself, even if it was for college. If I was lucky, I'd get into the local community college, but leaving home was out of the question.

Despite these discouragements, the fact remained: I was graduating high school. As the first in my family with a diploma of any kind, perhaps there was hope for a future beyond collecting social security.

Discovering My Roots

As physically fit and socially confident as I felt those last two years of high school, there were some hiccups along the way. Going into my senior year was especially difficult: my parents were in the midst of their big move, all of my friends were looking forward to college, and, on top of it all, I was having boy troubles.

My family's solution? "Ship the girl off to Italy!"

And so it came about that the summer before my senior year was spent in my father's hometown, learning smatterings of Italian, drinking sangria and rum and coke, and discovering what it meant to be a Belli.

The first day of my cross-continental journey, I woke up at the crack of dawn to bid my parents goodbye. My friends visited to whip up some of my favorite American food: steak, mashed potatoes, and corn (a far cry from my meals-to-come). Before I left, I made sure I told my parents how much I loved them.

"Your dad loves you, he just doesn't say it," my mother told me on my way out the door, hugging me farewell.

To understand my father, you need a little context: he immigrated to America from Patrica, Italy in his mid-20s. Although more members of the Belli family would eventually become Americans, for that first stretch of time, my father's sisters Rose and Nino were here and I only knew my cousins Marco and Sandro. I had never met my two younger cousins Sergio and Loredana. They were always like a dream. We would call Italy but we never believed they would actually move here. My dad met my mother through a friend soon after immigrating; she quickly went from being his English tutor to being his wife.

I was raised alongside my mother's Italian American cousins and siblings, all of whom were comfortably settled in America. But my father's family still stretched across the Atlantic; back in my father's home country lived an entire part of me that I had never met.

In many ways, I felt as distant from my father as I did my rural Italian roots. Any semblance of tenderness was hidden beneath a veneer of old-fashioned work ethic. I adored him from afar, constantly trying to elbow my way into his good graces – but I wasn't allowed to join him on his bricklaying projects ("You're a girl!" he would tell me, as if that explained anything). Despite this setback, I was always the first to volunteer when he had an errand to run or needed an extra hand, literally and figuratively.

My sisters and mother and I weren't afraid of my father, but he certainly always kept us on our toes. After a long day breaking concrete, he expected dinner on the table at 4:30 sharp. As soon as I caught a glimpse of my father's green truck pulling up to our house, I would speed home on my tiny bike, racing the clock to make sure the table was set before he removed his boots and work gear. "Bouya!" (*got you*) I would shout whenever I was scrambling to beat my father to the door, in the hopes that he wouldn't scold me for being late to set the table. After a long day working on scaffolds and repairing chimneys, he would be swathed in a semi-permanent coat of concrete and sweat which would mingle with the sweet aroma of marinara sauce coming from one of Mom's bubbling pots. We were not allowed to sit on the chairs in fear of ruining Mom's homemade pasta drying out on the beautifully draped linen towels. So, as I waited for Dad to be finished showering I would sneak in the bathroom and clean out my dad's pockets of change, he always had quarters and some dollar bills along with dirt from work. I always found it peaceful to roll his coins and cash them out. I was very fast to clean his pockets out, after all I had to compete with Maria but I was definitely faster and made an income doing this every night after Dad came home. And FYI, I always left the single bills.

My father also expected us to earn our keep. At 13, when I earned my very first babysitting paycheck, my father took one look at my earnings and told me, "Keep it coming."

"I don't get to keep it?"

"No, you have to contribute to the family."

It took a journey of more than 4,000 miles to finally understand the strange, quiet enigma that was my father.

Of course, I hadn't the slightest expectation of having a spiritual or familial epiphany when I was packing my suitcase. I just wanted to distract myself from a miserable break-up: "I'm going to move on and let him live his own life," I scribbled in my journal after a particularly devastating phone call with the boy in question. "Maybe, just maybe, I'll find a gorgeous Italian guy and I'll be rich and he'll take care of me and put a nice rock on my finger."

My trip to Italy was the perfect distraction, as it would turn out: Patrica was as different from my American lifestyle and adolescent woes as humanly possible. Patrica is a speck of a town, a rural community that takes up little more than a block of road. It's about 40 miles southeast of Rome – what Wikipedia describes as "an ancient hilltop commune (municipality) in the Province of Frosinone."

I was the first of my siblings to remember my dad's home country, so I had no point of reference, no one with whom I could speak candidly about what to expect. Luckily, I was joined by my Zia Rosina, who was traveling anyway and offered to bring me along, and my cousin Marco, who came as a favor to me ("you'll be bored out of your mind," he warned me).

When I arrived in Patrica, my father's attitudes toward money made immediate sense. This was an undeniably poor community, and the reality of my father having to be punished by my grandfather for stealing someone's eggs was very hard to understand. But work was far and few in Italy, and Dad had to come to America, he had a dream of building his own home. Leaving the family to find work was what did it. Despite my sisters' admonitions about our father's broken English – "He's lived in this country for so long! He has no excuse not to know the language!" – I suddenly understood firsthand how frustrating a language barrier could be. I was surprised by the vast cultural differences between Italy and America ("The people are very nice but don't sympathize for nobody," I noted in my journal about Italy), and could only imagine how challenging it must have been for my father in a strange country and at such a young age.

But what truly helped me understand my silent, self-sacrificing father was finally meeting his own father: Nonno.

I didn't remember my grandfather from his brief cohabitation in our home when I was very young, so upon meeting him, I was amazed to discover a man even more stoic and of fewer words than my father. When he wasn't working, my Nonno would spend hours sitting silently in his favorite chair, his lips pursed and his brows furrowed into what I called his "puss face." Despite his stoicism, Nonno was full of surprises. I distinctly remember giggling to myself the first time I saw him speed away on his moped, going 70 mph to pick up a jar of mayonnaise. And as he warmed up to me, his more outspoken side came out – usually in regards to my father.

"Tell your father to see me," he would spout.

"But Nonno, Dad's working all the time, it's hard for him to visit you."

"I haven't seen him in 14 years. I'll be dead before he comes!"

My step-grandmother was also a powerhouse, but she was nothing like my biological grandmother from what I was told. My biological grandmother was very nice and had died too young. She was in the United States some years earlier and was struck by a drunk driver outside of her church. My grandfather's new wife made it perfectly clear that I wasn't her real granddaughter, and she always seemed to have something to nag at me about, even if it was as innocent a mistake as leaving the windows open – something I was allowed to do back home because my parents' house had screened windows. I would later discover the flies that came in at night were brutal biters, as were the tarantula-sized mosquitoes.

I met a vast extended family across the ocean that summer. Much of my free time was spent bonding with my cousins and trying to live up to my tomboy reputation. My cousins were learning English, and their favorite comment whenever I did something particularly American was "you crazee!" They convinced me that I might have been lucky to have grown up with bickering sisters after all; their arguments were mostly relegated to insults and screaming. My male cousins, on the other hand, loved to challenge me to games of Frog, which involved punching each other's arms until our welts turned up and would go down again. Still, I learned to love my new relatives, and appreciated their generosity as they welcomed me into their homes and introduced me to this new, beautiful world.

Italy itself was stunning, with sunny afternoons and sticky-sweet nights. I roamed the countryside, discovering lemons the size of grapefruits and roasting hazelnuts in the sun after picking them straight from the tree. I loved going to the beach with my cousins, where the water was pure and clear enough that I could see grooves in the sand beneath my toes. My body crisped into a golden brown, but not after peeling from so much sun and recovering from the onslaught of mosquitoes (I made the mistake of wearing perfume outside early in my visit). After a long, sweat cleansing day outdoors, my cousins and I would treat ourselves to refreshing gelato, licking our fingers as the sun set for the day.

Whenever possible, my relatives took me on outings, from the local "American bar," which included a one-lane bowling alley, to the dance-filled festival of Saint Anna. We went to Rome and Naples and drank from the "Fountain of Youth" in Fiuggi. My favorite adventure by far was to the sulfur pool. I was skeptical about bathing in such putrid-smelling water at first (comparing sulfur to rotten eggs is almost being insulting to eggs), but as soon as I took my first dip, I was obsessed. The water was soothing from the inside out. Week after week, I begged to return, as if my body and spirit were craving a kind of deep purification that was impossible to find in America. I would learn later that doctors prescribe sulfur water as part of a medicinal regime. Drinking this rotten egg concoction was not as exciting as swimming, but I am still called back to the pools til this day…

Before my month was up, my family made sure to take me to Vallepietra Sanctuary Italy Santissima Trinita in Vallepietra, a town on the Apennine mountains, near Rome. Miracles happen and the sick are cured: this is where, more than a decade ago, my aunt/zia Rosina had walked up the shrine's many steps with no shoes, backwards, praying that my "predicted mortality of 90%" would be proven wrong. At the top of the steps, I was amazed to discover crutches and other discarded mementoes from pain and sickness that had been cured through prayer. I may not have been convinced that a higher power had been the one to save me from my early brush with death, but seeing the lengths to which my distant family went to pray for my recovery moved me to the core.

Even more special to me than the sulfur springs and shrine of miracles, however, was the new family that I had grown to love. The trip back to the airport was bittersweet, as I noted in my journal:

I tried to hold my tears, but just when I said goodbye they all came out. I really miss him and I hope he's around for a while so I can come back again. So far we had arguments and a lot of tears. He's a very stubborn man but has a big heart. I can't wait to see my father; they look exactly alike.

The last entry in my journal from that month is a list entitled *Things to Never Forget*:

- Nonno in his chair with that puss on his face
- Eat more, that's alright
- Zia Diamira and her little bad remarks that will make you pee your pants
- Zia Rosa telling me I don't eat enough, don't sleep, clean up after yourself.
- Little Marco always calling me crazy (moti)
- Nello saying "you're crazy"
- Mariucci's Little Mario Belli's red face, saying I should have a beer or sangria peach in wine
- Cezar getting me with the flash of the camera and him saying schizophrenic with Emma.
- Zia Pierina-Stellina she would call me
- Marra and my other friends in Supino where we celebrate San Cataldo, the patron saint of Supino, Italy.
- Emma making faces at Cezar behind his back
- My cousins the twins and my cousin who studied in Rome
- Zio Americo: what a sweet guy, always smiling in his stark white t-shirt

Being home after a month of learning new words and meeting new family members felt surreal. I was ecstatic to reunite with my girlfriends, and I certainly didn't have a certain boy on my mind any more. But most importantly, I was relieved to see my father again, puttering around the garden and barking orders in his thick Italian accent. He wasn't some strange, imposing figure anymore, but a real person, and someone I could truly understand.

Need a lift? I have my Herman Munster shoes on with the length on the interior and exterior equaling 3 inches - they were great when I had them but definitely temporary.

A gym award

Post leg surgery photo. My fantasy photo: California dreaming and wanting to attend Pepperdine University.

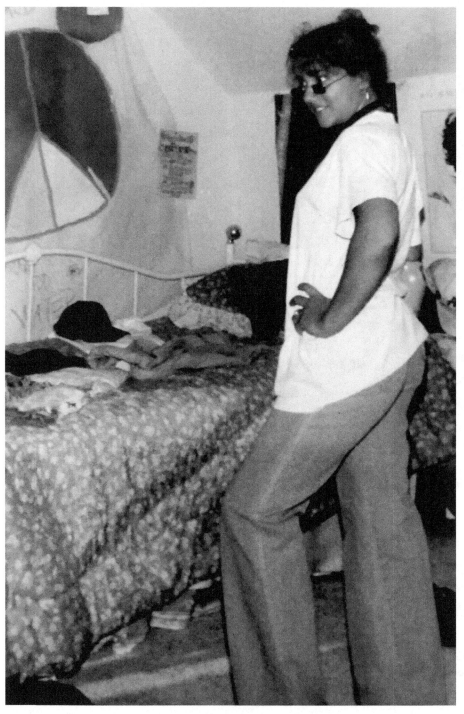

South Carolina visiting my girl, Medea. I miss you!

Our famous trip to Italy in 1992.

Zia Rose, you are an amazing cook! I miss you, Zia Pierina.

Most of my cousins when I visited Italy.

Nonno, so cute and stoic.

Dad before coming to Italy back in the day.

Zio Orlando, Nonno, and Dad together in our old home;
good days always around a table.

My cousins, Lore and Sergio, from Italy, that are finally in America.
You were like a brother and sister to me. Love you guys!

My graduation from high school.

3

THE TUMORS

Love and Independence

Italy filled me with a reinvigorated love for my family's culture, for sweet vine-ripe green and red tomatoes, and for travel. Prior to my Patrica adventure, my first adventures had been to visit relatives in Montreal, followed by a trip to (and subsequent love affair with) California. Now that I'd finished high school and was an official adult, this was the optimal time to take a journey by myself.

Against my parents' wishes – they strongly disapproved of traveling without a familial chaperone – I traveled to South Carolina to visit my friend Medea: "A graduation gift from me to me," I noted in my travel journal. I miss you Medea.

I enjoyed independence to its fullest. I reveled in the lack of parental supervision, dancing late into the night, getting tipsy with friends, even getting a tattoo ("I can't believe I did it! Miss Angela Belli, we did it!" I wrote). I was of age after all. I jotted down highlights of my trip, from partying at an LGBT bar and eating lots of fried food to renting risqué movies and learning to drive standard ("not bad for a girl on the street with one arm"). My parents would have been mortified.

But my first taste of freedom wasn't all nightclubs and beach trips. Homesickness set in even before the plane to Raleigh left the ground:

As I sit here gathering my thoughts, I can still remember my father's expression as I left the house at six this morning. It was a very cold and hated expression, but nothing out of the ordinary. As for my mother, well, she's too much. She takes care of me better than any father and mother I know. I love her very much and can't tell her that all the time. But I do think she knows that I wish her only the best and that she needs to lighten the hand holding, just a bit.

Back at home, I was torn: I had missed my parents dearly while away, but Connecticut felt small and stagnant compared to the warm, beachy atmospheres of California and South Carolina. Despite my reservations, however, I didn't see a way out of my parents' house, so I caved: I elected to receive social security. I was certainly eligible, and it would have been the perfect plan for someone whose needs and personality differed from mine. But I was too stubborn, too ambitious, too passionate about life to stay at home for days on end. After mere few months of collecting social security and sinking into a miserable depression, I made plans to find work.

I'd babysat in high school, along with a few other odd jobs – working as a restroom attendant, a coat girl, a page girl at our local library, even as a housekeeper – but this new chapter in my life required work that was more substantial. I first found myself slicing meat at a deli and crafting drinks at a coffee shop. I was on my feet all day, but the thrill of bringing home a paycheck every week made the long hours worthwhile; I love working.

I was still living with my parents and paying about $100 in rent a month, but our new house was much calmer than our claustrophobic old two-bedroom. Carla had long since moved out to live with her husband and daughter (my first godchild), although I still babysat and played with my beloved niece as often as possible. Maria was still living with us – and she was about to break our comfortable, quiet little household wide open.

Maria and I were closer in age than Carla and I, so she took it upon herself to mentor me in the ways of womanhood: most importantly, the art of flirting and dancing. Maria loved taking me to nightclubs, where I fell passionately in love with the neon lights and heart-pumping music.

I was nervous about these outings at first; I wasn't wearing a prosthesis the very first time Maria brought me with her, so I remember standing in the corner awkwardly as my sister was asked to dance by boy after boy after boy. I was terrified of stepping onto the dance floor without a hand, so I contented myself to just watch. But when my prosthesis came in, it was as if I'd received a new pair of feet as well: I craved the nightlife and never wanted to stop dancing.

Maria and I met all sorts of glamorous people, going as far as New York to discover the best DJs and music and dance partners. I remember the two of us falling so in love with a particular record that we searched every store in town for a copy, to no avail – only to finally hear the original cover again at a nightclub for kids 18 and up. We were ecstatic, and we danced all night long. One night, we wanted to go out so badly that we lied to our dad and saved money for a cab. When we finally arrived, I leapt from the car and onto the street, only for the driver to run over my foot. "Back up, back up!" I hollered from outside, not because of the pain but because I was missing out on all the fun happening inside: I was dying to go to that nightclub.

One fateful night, Maria got a little carried away with the festivities and found herself too drunk to make her way home alone. We'd just become acquainted with a near-stranger named Dante (his real name was Matt); I anxiously asked for help. "Excuse me Dante, but my sister drank too much tonight. Can you bring us home? We live right around the corner but this car can't stay overnight in this parking lot; my dad will kill us."

Five months later, my sister was sitting on the living room couch downing a bag of potato chips in front of the television.

"What's wrong with you?" my father asked. "You look like a whale."

"So?" my sister replied.

"What, are you pregnant or something?"

"Actually I am."

My father and I were struck silent. Maria hadn't spoken a word to me about what had happened with Matt that night months earlier, let alone about being *pregnant*. This, of course, was completely against our traditional Catholic code of values – but there was nothing to be done. Four months later, my second niece and goddaughter was born. I was blamed for introducing her parents, and although Maria refused to marry Matt, we consider him our estranged Italianish (he loves mom's food, too) brother-in-law and we welcome him into our family. I was delighted to babysit Gabbi while my sister worked, reveling in my aunthood status once again.

Little did I know that I would be the next Belli daughter to rock the boat.

My luck with men had been middling at best by this point. I hadn't been dating for particularly long, but the boyfriends and flings I'd had were more than enough to make me jaded towards romance. I still had a bad habit of putting too much trust into others, so relationships more often than not ended with heartbreak on my end.

All this to say that when one of my girlfriends insisted on introducing me to a "really nice guy," I was more than a bit skeptical.

"I've had my share of 'nice guys,'" I told her. "They're all nice until they do something wrong."

"Just meet this one," she said. "Trust me."

My friend invited me to her house where she planned to casually introduce us. *Hoffa* was playing on the television and, sure enough, a young Italian man was sitting on the couch with some friends, saying every word of dialogue by heart as they came out of Jack Nicholson's mouth.

Massimo, I learned, was a Teamster himself, so Jimmy Hoffa was a hero for him.

"This is my movie, this is my boss! Jimmy Hoffa!" he cheered. To my surprise, he was comforting to talk to. I quickly felt at ease sitting next to this stranger. He had a laid-back sense of humor and I soon found myself laughing at his quips. I was having a better time than I could have imagined until the dreaded subject arose:

"What's wrong with your hand?" Massimo asked, noticing my prosthesis.

"You don't know?" I cried. "Nobody told you?"

I turned to his friend Vinnie. "You didn't tell him I have one arm?"

"That's not funny. You shouldn't joke like that."

I turned to Massimo, perplexed.

"What do you mean?"

"That's not something you should joke about," Massimo replied. "People who get injured – it's not funny."

I was astounded. No one had ever reacted to my hand in such a sensitive way. I'd become immune to snide remarks about my disability, so I was floored to hear someone take it so seriously. It was quite refreshing.

It turns out that Massimo was as traditional as he was kind-hearted. For our first date, I begged him to park around the block so he wouldn't have to interact with my parents; Maria was far along in her pregnancy at this point, and I was terrified that my father would murder the next man who threatened to besmirch one of his daughters. Massimo, however, had no intention of committing any impropriety, insisting on courting me properly. My father opened the door to Massimo's polite knocks and interrogated him with his razor-sharp glare before speaking.

"What's your name?"

"Massimo."

"You speak Italian?"

"Yes, sir."

My date and I held our breaths as my father considered his final verdict.

"*Stai attento* (be careful)," he warned. "Have her home by eleven."

"Eleven!" I thought to myself, disappointed. If he had dropped me off on the corner I could have at least stayed out until the clubs closed. Despite the curfew, I had permission to go on my first, official, father-approved date. Massimo was not content to take me out for a cheap meal, either; true to his gentlemanly persona, he escorted me to an evening at the casino, where I watched him light up with every little victory at the roulette. It was a perfect night out, and although I would eventually become Massimo's gambling conscience

("You've won enough, don't push it: that's going in our savings account"), this first glimpse into his thrill-seeking side was exhilarating.

We dated for a year and a half before becoming engaged, and waited another year and a half to get married. I needed the extra time to plan: this was to be the dream wedding to end all dream weddings, after all.

Of course, no event in my life would be complete without some kind of medical emergency: in the midst of wedding preparations, I inquired about pain in my knee and was informed that I had a torn meniscus. I had arthroscopic surgery six months before walking down the aisle, leading to last-minute dress fittings and the elimination of my gorgeous runner – but nothing could stop me from having the wedding of my dreams. Italian weddings are no small affairs to begin with, but I wanted as much extravagance and largesse as possible for my big day. Family arrived from across the country and the Atlantic, an elegant dinner and venetian table was served, and my dress was a lacy, trailing, hip-hugging thing of beauty, straight out of a bridal catalogue.

As excited as I was to finally strike out on my own and start a life with Massimo, leaving home proved painful. My sister and niece had been living with us for a few years by then, and I was heartbroken to move away from my godchild. I certainly didn't have my mother's cooking skills, so our newlywed apartment wouldn't have the constant aroma of tomato sauce and vegetable soup (even my coworkers loved poking fun at my culinary ineptitude, so I actually received a collection of recipes as a work shower gift).

In the airport terminal on our way to our honeymoon, I jotted down all my fears and joys:

- Massimo and I are sitting in an Air Jamaica terminal and I just had a few things come to mind.
- First, I can't stop thinking of my mom and dad and how much they have done for me. I love them both so much. I feel like I am empty and sad right now because I am not with them. I know it is time for me to let go but I am very close to them and I love them both so much, it chokes me up just thinking about it....
- I pray to God that we have a healthy and full life together, and yes, maybe we will have children in like five years or more. Massimo is looking at all the planes taking off, he looks like a little kid in a candy store. The sun looks like it is going to come out soon.
- As life-changing as my marriage was, it was marked with unforgettable milestones, many of which I reflected upon with our one year anniversary:
- Our first breakfast together felt like we were still on our honeymoon.
- Our first fight we were mad but willing to forgive each other.
- Our first Christmas Eve we were saddened by the loss of my grandfather but we went over to my Zia Rose's and were trying to be happy, because Nonno always wanted

the family to be together. We decorated the threshold with garland and lights. We decorated the tree in a deep burgundy, we hung up our stockings, put up a fresh tree and had a quiet but happy first Christmas Eve.

- Our first Valentine's we went to Anthony's Ocean View for a dinner/dance and had a great time – we seem to meet a lot of engaged couples – we are glad we are married.
- Our first vacation we went to Myrtle Beach.
- Our first anniversary – spent in a beautiful condo in the Cayman Island. Had a ball! (maybe even better than honeymoon). It was not inexpensive but it was unforget-table. We have the pictures to prove it! Massimo thought I rented the island. It was full of pink sand and swings from palm trees – truly beautiful.

Those first few trips were nothing compared to the adventures Massimo and I would have over the years. I made sure to instill in my new husband the same love of travel I had developed – starting with our first stay in New York City.

Massimo was confused at first. Why were we traveling without our group of friends? What kind of fun could we have by ourselves? After some cajoling, I finally convinced him to journey down to the city, just the two of us, where we stayed in a closet-sized hotel room in the center of everything. I took it upon myself to educate my husband on the art of being a tourist.

"Whatever you do, don't take out your map," I instructed. "You'll be a walking target."

"But how will we know how to get anywhere?"

"We'll ask for directions or something. We'll figure it out, don't worry about it!"

Sure enough, the first thing he did after exiting the subway was pull out his map. I was forgiving enough: after all, this was his first big trip, and he was clearly nervous. After a few nights on the town, however, complete with drinking and eating and dancing, everything clicked for Massimo. Pretty soon, he was the planner and keeper of our travel itineraries and I the wide-eyed tagalong.

These days, the two of us make a point of leaving the States as frequently as possible. We love the warmth throughout the rest of the world, both in temperature and personality: people elsewhere, even as near as the West Coast, are so much kinder and more open-minded (at its best, Connecticut is pretty; at its worst, it's cold, clammy, and full of cranky New Englanders). We love getting tours from locals, sampling new cuisines, and looking at the world from a new perspective.

Our cross-continental adventures have been many – and our love affair with travel and romance all began during that magical first year of marriage.

Back to School (and Waiting Rooms)

Of course, as wonderful as our first year together had been, nothing stays simple for long. Soon after our wedding, Massimo received news that the Stop and Shop warehouse where he worked would be moving to upstate New York. The message was clear: in a few years at most, my husband would soon be out of a job.

"Move back home!" my parents rejoiced. "You can have your old room back!"

I was humiliated. Here we were, in our first apartment – cozy and simple but all ours – and my parents wanted me to give up my independence to rely on them again. Massimo stuck out his job for a few years, as long as he could; in the meantime, he and I considered our options and realized that, as much as this news felt like a loss, it could also present a marvelous opportunity.

I had always dreamt of moving to North Haven. The town of West Haven where I had grown up was quaint, but cramped and messy: everyone lived a block away from each other and all your neighbors knew your cousins and friends, you could never escape the noise. In comparison, North Haven felt like a country club. Best of all, it boasted a great school system – perfect for the children Massimo and I were considering having.

And so it was that we found ourselves touring a house in North Haven. This should have been a dream come true, but for one tiny problem: I hated the house.

"It has good bones," said my father, the bricklayer and self-proclaimed expert. "Good location, good structure. You change the floors, clean it up, it's perfect."

But the house was on the wrong side of the city, where the schools weren't quite as nice – and, of course, it was out of our price range. Massimo and I followed our realtor's advice and put down an offer, just in case. When we got the phone call that our offer had been accepted, the house didn't seem quite as distasteful to me anymore. In an instant, I went from skeptical to ecstatic.

Our new home was, in many ways, everything that my childhood home wasn't: it had extra bedrooms (one for a nursery, we imagined), plenty of space, a fenced-in yard, even room for an elegant dining table. It wasn't my dream house, but it would become my dream home.

The first thing I said to my friends and family after moving in was that I would have a bucket next to the front door. It wouldn't be for ice, though: I would instead ask any and all guests to dump all garbage and sadness and anger in the bucket before entering my home. This would be a peaceful space, a safe haven away from all the messiness and drama of the outside world.

Here I was, zipping through life and checking off milestone after milestone along the way. As all of these massive changes were happening in my personal life, however, my professional life was stagnating.

After bouncing around from job to job those first few years out of high school, I finally landed work that seemed like it might have some upward mobility. A temp agency placed me at GIST, Inc., a prepress company that made film from graphics in New Haven. The company hired me full-time as a receptionist, and at first, I was thrilled to finally be stretching my brain and learning new skills. Along with greeting clients in person and over the phone, I found myself in charge of data entry and accounts receivable, as well as whatever other administrative tasks crossed my desk. Soon, however, I hit a wall.

This was a wall I would encounter many times over throughout my professional career. I always made myself an invaluable employee, arriving early and leaving late, taking on extra tasks, doing whatever it took to make my team happy. I earned praise from my coworkers and supervisors, but their praise never extended beyond empty words of gratitude. I would never get fired, certainly, but I would also never get promoted.

Part of this workhorse mentality stemmed from a fear of letting people down should a health emergency rear its ugly head. What if I missed days or weeks or months of work? I needed to clock in as many hours of hard work now in case I would lose them in the future.

Given my life experiences, this paranoia wasn't entirely unfounded. One of my most embarrassing memories took place when I was recovering from Lyme disease. I was spearheading an important public event, meaning that I was in charge of everything from hiring staff to setting up and breaking down. If anything, I was over prepared for the big day, but the morning of, I was so exhausted that I was literally incapable of lifting my head from my pillow. My husband and sister volunteered to help and ensure that the event ran smoothly, but I was mortified. Here I was, entrusted with an important project, of which I was perfectly capable of managing, only to be struck down with yet another medical emergency when it truly mattered. I couldn't fathom how I would ever get hired for a job with real responsibility, no matter how impeccable my resume.

As luck would have it, the early years of my career would be marked by a fair share of medical milestones. First was the most seemingly innocuous of the lot: carpal tunnel syndrome. For most people, carpal tunnel is inconvenient, but an easy fix: a wrist brace or surgery is more than sufficient. For me, however, having impaired use of my left hand was as major an impediment as I could suffer, and the prospect of having surgery on my one remaining hand was an utter nightmare.

I didn't need a doctor to tell me why my hand was such a wreck. Soon after high school, I'd gotten in a car accident, during which I squeezed the wheel more tightly than I thought possible. When my fingers started going numb, the connection was clear. I remember working in the deli and watching salami slip out of my limp left hand – but despite the clear evidence that something was wrong, I avoided my doctor at all costs.

The idea of doing any kind of procedure on my one remaining hand was too much to comprehend, so I fell into a habit I would return to time and again: I ignored my body's signals and just kept working.

Finally, after a full two years of suffering, I surrendered to the pain. I started receiving cortisone shots, but nothing did the trick. Eventually, the pain started shooting all the way up to my neck, at which point the doctors and I knew something more drastic needed to happen. Luckily, my doctor was as wary as I about causing unnecessary harm to my single hand. Neither of us wanted to do invasive surgery in case it went even the slightest bit wrong. My doctor eventually cut my hand open instead of using lasers, for fear of accidentally hitting something. This prospect still terrified me, but posed the fewest risks.

It's funny to reflect on how much ire was caused by a seemingly harmless setback like carpal tunnel syndrome. It seems silly, but in all honesty, it was one of the scariest experiences of my life up until that point: as much as I was used to life with a prosthesis, I couldn't imagine being without my left hand. The entire ordeal was a frightening reminder of how my disability can transform even the smallest of challenges into the most petrifying of emergencies.

In a much-deserved twist of fate, my next major health emergency seemed to be little more than a false alarm. I was 24-ish years old when I noticed my feet going numb. While jogging with a coworker, the numbness intensified so that it cramped up my entire foot. An MRI revealed two, olive-sized tumors in the middle of my spine. I was diagnosed with ependymomas – benign tumors – and the treatment was astoundingly straightforward: the tumors were removed, no complications arose, and I was told they would never come back. I completed my associate's degree, and life returned to normal – for a few years, at least.

In between medical emergencies, work continued as usual. I worked tirelessly, got a pat on the back for my effort, and started all over again. I was happy enough, but undeniably stuck.

"What makes an employee vital?" I wanted to know. "How can I prove that I'm more than just a workhorse?" According to various Rehabilitation Services, there was only one answer: Education. I was once told that in order to finally climb in the ranks and build a career, I had to go back to school for my associate's degree.

I was petrified. I had been out of school for nearly a decade and certainly didn't have any familial mentors who could provide guidance or advice.

"What do you want to go to school for?" my father asked. "Only stupid people who don't know what they want to do go to school."

College was a foreign concept to the Belli family, so I would have to pave the way alone.

Surprisingly, college started off not as the intellectually rigorous minefield I expected, but as a nurturing, creative environment. In one of my introductory classes, we watched *The Wizard of Oz* and were prompted to draw pictures of the film and reflect on how fear needn't be an impediment to chasing our dreams; you have the power to do anything. As an art project, we were asked to consider what part of a flower we were at that moment in our lives: the strong but invisible root, the blossoming flower, or somewhere in between? I was even asked to consider my "biggest fears or concerns" and how they might affect my non-school life:

My biggest concerns as I begin college are my health. I don't know whether or not I'll have to miss school due to future surgeries. I have a deteriorating knee and I've always missed a lot of school due to my many illnesses. I hope I know when to ask questions and when to figure things out on my own. I hope my family can put up with me. I'm very involved in my nieces' lives and have to watch them on a regular basis. I hope they don't get bored in the library. My fears are also that I may not find a job, even with a degree, due to prejudices. I have been denied employment before – in fact, the only way I could find my current job was through a temping agency. I find that even professional people have a hard time hiring me. I hope I can find a job with a degree and that people can see past my disabilities.

Soon into my collegiate career, I rediscovered something I had forgotten since graduating from high school: I love learning. I love asking questions, exploring new ideas, stretching my brain and meeting with new mentors. As passionate as I was about school, however, I assumed that my associate's degree

in Business Management would be the end of that journey –
and I couldn't have been more wrong.

Despite the degree, I was trapped in the same, never-ending
cycle of drudge work. I expected the world to open up to me
after my degree, for opportunities to present themselves and
job offers to come pouring in. After my husband and I moved,
I ended up getting a job closer to home as a Switchboard
Operator at Town Hall – an exciting change, but not one that
offered the intellectual stimulation or growth opportunities
I craved.

Aside from prejudice and my workhorse mentality, one of
the other reasons I felt stuck at work was because I shirked from
requesting accommodations, no matter how many problems
they could have solved. I was well out of high school by this
point, but I still clung to the safety of being invisible. At best,
pointing out my need for different accommodations would
call attention to my being different; at worst, it would make
me seem needy and high-maintenance. I was able to provide
some materials myself, such as the cushioned pens I needed
after my carpal tunnel surgery. Others, like an electric stapler,
I was too embarrassed to request; informing my manager that
a manual stapler strained my hand was out of the question. I
also avoided asking for the expensive Infogrip BAT keyboard,
a one-handed keyboard that helps people with physical
impairments type with comfort and speed. Eventually, one of
my managers demanded I receive an electric stapler, as well as
a better-sized chair that would help with my neuropathy in my

legs. I've since become more outspoken about my needs, but at this early stage in my career, I preferred to stay quiet and accommodating – even if that silence held me back.

Many years ago now, I asked for advice from a friend of mine who happened to also be a finance director, and he encouraged me to enter the field of finance. "Another degree?" I thought to myself.

"You need to do something that's universal," he told me. "A degree in finance is going to be helpful in any area of your life."

"But I've never been good at math," I said.

"It's not about math. It's about planning. You have programs to take care of the math. You're thinking about the future."

In an unexpected way, finances aligned with my worldview. I would have made a terrible accountant, a field that involves a live-in-the-moment perspective. Financial planning, on the other hand, is about thinking long-term with your eyes constantly on the horizon. For better or worse, I tend to have my brain thinking towards the future rather than the present, so the idea of using that mindset to further my career was tantalizing.

Sure enough, I fell in love with learning all over again. One of my favorite classes wasn't in finances at all, but in humanities. I had a brilliant professor who encouraged us to read texts in an in-depth, critical way that cracked open the world of reading for me. The class focused in particular on the life and writings of Martin Luther King, Jr. I knew King's story, of course, but had never studied it with the depth and breadth that was required of our class, an exercise that encouraged me to look at other people's experiences through a more intimate perspective. In another lifetime, I would have gone for my master's in humanities, but I wasn't able to find a practical way to integrate that field of study into my professional life. That person-focused mindset did, however, refocus my long-term career path from one of financial support towards one of advocacy.

I was enjoying college, but life can always find a way to complicate things. For me, of course, these complications are usually in the form of hospital visits. A year into school, my husband and I were browsing for Christmas presents at the mall when I felt an excruciating pain shoot through my foot. I had a feeling that bad news was en route. I ignored the sinking feeling that I needed to see a specialist and saw a podiatrist, who confirmed the worst of my fears: I needed an oncologist's help.

Despite promises to the contrary, my tumors were back, possibly benign but possibly cancerous, and this time there was one mass in my foot as well as reoccurring ones in my spine. The foot surgery was a breeze, taking me out of work for a day at most; I was walking again in no time. The spine surgery was another story entirely.

The surgery itself would take me out of work for about a month, on top of which I would need radiation to dispel the tumors in my back. Radiation is an ordeal for anyone, but I also faced fertility risks due to where the radiation beam would be impacting my body. After getting a second opinion once again from Johns Hopkins (and dining on some divine blue crabs), I opted to freeze one of my ovaries instead of pursuing in-vitro-fertilization. By the time I went in for radiation, one of my ovaries was being stored at Cornell (where it still resides) and the other had been moved up and out of the radiation area.

Motherhood had always been a vague concept to me, something I hadn't considered at any length until my fertility was on the line. Even though I wasn't sure if I wanted to have children, the prospect of never being able to conceive was devastating. In my overflowing family of mothers and aunts and daughters, bearing children was an assumed part of every woman's life; this, compounded with the fact that all of my friends were having children at the time, left me feeling isolated and ashamed.

As I grappled with these notions of identity and purpose, some of my friends rejected me outright. I was used to seeing the uglier side of people when I was sick, but this massive falling out hurt more than I could have anticipated. Instead of trying to understand my pain and struggles with fertility, my friends – many of whom were new mothers – balked at my struggles, even calling me selfish for being emotionally distant and needing to grapple with my own issues.

I loved my two goddaughters more than I could express, but I had to turn down an offer from a cousin of mine because of how the birth lined up with my own fertility issues.

When another offer to be godmother came my way, I knew I needed to take the opportunity and force myself to change for the better. The christening of my new godchild was one of the hardest afternoons of my life, a daylong internal battle between happiness for this new family and self-pity over the fear of never holding a child of my own. Photos of the day show me with a forced smile and short hair, for once, an external change that I hoped would spur an internal spark of happiness. I was surrounded by cousins and relatives glowing with pride while I struggled to hold back tears.

When I thought logically, I knew that my troubles were minor in the grand scheme of things. I was getting radiation alongside a man with brain cancer who was also a father of three, a burden that must have weighed on him heavily. At any point he could fall asleep, have a seizure, and not wake up – but every time I saw him, he had a smile on his face. I couldn't fathom where he found that kind of power. I ached for the ability to grin and bear my own struggles, but some days were much harder than others. Even now, when I am in a place of relative stability and on a clear path to physical recovery, there are mornings when getting out of bed is an immeasurable challenge. I like to say that I get out of bed just for spite – to prove that I'm alive and can still conquer anything. This is a mindset I've worked hard to attain, and I certainly hadn't nailed it in my early 30s.

I had plenty of physical pain to accompany these emotional challenges. With radiation came an onslaught of symptoms:

the treatment exhausted my spinal column and dried out my nerves, I had trouble walking, and I blew up from the medicine I was being administered. I was also being prescribed innumerable drugs to put my body and mind back on track. All while I was going through hormonal changes and adjusting to the steroids, which made me very fidgety.

When I later worked at a mental health clinic, I would learn that many of the drugs that the oncologists were prescribing me were contradictory. Some were necessary to reduce inflammation, for instance, but they ended up causing anxiety; the medication meant to ease that anxiety would help in the short-term but cause my nerves to flare up once the effects wore off. I was caught in a vicious cycle: I needed certain medications to heal my body, but didn't want to become reliant on this never-ending path from one drug to another to another.

Wary of long-term side effects and reliance on drugs, I turned to alternative remedies. For relaxation, I tapped into meditation and yoga; I practiced mindfulness, which helped me concentrate on the here and now rather than fears of what was to come. I learned that ice is a miracle drug and hot showers anger my nerves. A pain management doctor even introduced me to acupuncture and cupping. Soon enough, I was lying face-down with needles covering what looked like every inch of my body, and I felt for the first time in ages as if I was truly being healed. I learned that I needed to open up my meridians to release energy and recover from the inside-out. My insurance didn't cover as much treatment as I needed, but even a limited number of sessions was a blessing.

I missed about a semester of school altogether. I was in an accelerated program, so it was easy enough to jump back on board the following term, although I wasn't able to graduate with my original group of peers. In the meantime, my hiatus from school seemed to stretch on for years instead of months. To get out of the house, I sought volunteer opportunities, ways to contribute to the community and expand my world beyond hospital walls.

Inspired by my early experiences working with senior citizens, I went through a rigorous training program to work with hospice patients. I was only assigned one patient, and I had the sneaking suspicion once again that prejudice was at the root of this problem. Luckily, even my one assignment was life-changing in and of itself. I was sent to the bedside of an elderly woman whose family no longer lived nearby; during the few times I visited her before she passed, I held her hand, prayed, read to her, and kept her company. It was gratifying to realize that my many experiences interacting with doctors and patients, however exhausting they had been for me, could have a healing effect on others.

Yet again, the press picked up on my story. This time, the headline declared, "Woman Fights Illness with Optimism." In the photo, I have a broad smile, the switchboard phone at my ear, putting on a show of happiness and hard work as usual. It was the image I projected and lived by at the time: ignore the pain, get paid, and move on.

My in-laws and my husband. We will never forget you.

La Familia in Italy.

Nonni and Nonno, we miss you!

My family in Canada. We love you!

Thank you, Uncle Jimmy, for always looking out for me – I love you!

*A taste for dancing at the Chalet in Villa Roma on a family trip with
both sides of my family.*

My dance buddy, partner in crime, bestie, and cousin, Joyce. You are a rock! Thank you for always being supportive; love you!

Just before my wedding, I was squeezing my niece, Gab, who called everyone "mommy." I never minded, but when I corrected her to call me Auntie Angela, she would call me Eia instead.

*One of the most glorious and emotional days of my life with my
Godchild, Sophia, and my cousin, Pam. You are so special to
me and I love you both.*

4

BUILDING MUSCLE

More School (More Waiting Rooms)

After years of feeling like I was being held captive on some kind of never-ending hospital carousel – checking in and out, in and out, year after year – I graduated with my B.A. and did something I never expected: I entered the world of healthcare voluntarily.

In retrospect, this path makes perfect sense. Who knows more about the ins and outs of hospitals than a patient, particularly one who has undergone so many types of treatments? A master's degree in Healthcare Management was also a callback to my love for the humanities: a people-centered approach to a world that is far too often devoid of bedside manners and personal care. I had grown up in hospitals and waiting rooms, this was my chance to improve these experiences for people like me.

I matriculated into Cambridge College's Healthcare Management program, a mix of online and classroom studies, giving me the flexibility to continue working. My body, as usual, seemed to revolt against my academic goals, but my brain was undeterred. Along with the knowledge to guide future patients through the often-debilitating world of hospital care, I gained invaluable mentorship from my peers and instructors. Professor Shircliff, in particular, comes to mind. I was a bundle of nerves entering her classroom, as I'd heard plenty of whispers about how tough she could be on her students. To my amazement, she was more dedicated and well-rounded than many of the teachers I'd had before her. Through her, I learned about risk-reduction, the idea of offering preventative care to keep patients out of hospitals to begin with, and many more lessons on policy and procedure.

Of course, this was advice I should have been taking myself. I was grateful for the alternative, drug-free treatments I had discovered during radiation, but I had yet to integrate those mindfulness and self-care techniques into my everyday life. I still preferred to ignore pain and put others before myself, even at the gamble of my own exhaustion.

My master's program was also an opportunity to expand what it means to care for a community. Continuing my passion for caring for the elderly, I applied for and received a grant from New Haven to start a program called Mental Health Making Waves. I partnered senior citizens with senior high schoolers; the older seniors taught patience, while the younger seniors taught technical skills. I was awarded 13 iPads, which the teenagers used to help the senior citizens communicate with family members across the country. My mother was my guinea pig, going from complaining that she couldn't find the on button to becoming addicted to FaceTime. The program continues to this day, and despite some ongoing challenges (namely getting affordable WiFi to seniors), I take pride in knowing that I made a difference in lives young and old.

Around the same time that I went back for my third advanced degree, I started emerging from my shell of invisibility. For years, I had hidden in the background – from not speaking up in school to pretending I didn't need special accommodations at work – but college had challenged that mindset. In order to succeed in higher education, I was required to be vocal, to ask questions, and to stand up for myself. This new outlook started bleeding into my world outside of school as well.

I loved volunteering, but the challenges I faced with such work were similar to those at school: important milestones seemed to always align with medical emergencies. Ever since my early days dunking people at the local carnival, I had sought opportunities to help people and organizations in need. I helped out at the Branford Soup Kitchen, dropping off food or cooking on-sight, a nod to my Italian culinary roots and my mother's joy of feeding throngs of hungry relatives. Throughout my life as an amputee, electronics have become my hands and feet, and whenever I was wheelchair or hospital bed bound, computers have been my windows to the rest of the world – a passion for technology and business led to my work with our local Chamber of Commerce.

Now that I was earning my master's degree, I decided to work with the League of Women voters, making phone calls and running informational booths at fairs. I was even featured in a televised infomercial encouraging residents to exercise their right to vote. But as I became increasingly involved with the League, I became increasingly anxious as well.

You see, there was a pattern to my volunteer work. I would join an organization, nervous and excited. I would get to know the community and staff and earn my usual reputation as a reliable workhorse. I would bravely nominate myself to take on a leadership position or additional responsibility. Then as soon as I would move out of my comfort zone for that next big step, I would fall ill. This happened as early as junior high school, when I was elected to my student council, only to miss that entire year for my leg surgery. So naturally, when I heard about a big opportunity as a Connecticut delegate, I was wary: who would want a jinx like me in such an important role?

Miraculously, my work as a delegate didn't end in a rush to the hospital or weary resignation from my hospital bedside. Instead, I became enthralled by the patriotism and citizenship that surrounded me. I even made another television appearance that managed to impress even my father, who had earned his citizenship a few years prior. This next step in my advocacy work – from smaller organizations to state citizenship – was inspiring. I learned about the voting process on an intimate level, but I also blossomed as a leader and community volunteer. I used my voice in a way that 15-year-old Angela would have never dreamed possible.

Of course, this new stage of life wouldn't be complete unless it were interrupted by another health crisis. Around the summer of 2014, I was doing my regular physical exam in the shower – a habit I've developed over the years, probably from the trauma with my leg and spine tumors – and noticed a lump in one of my breasts. As usual, I suppressed all fear and self-pity, even any suspicion that something might be wrong. There was no history of breast cancer in my family, after all, so surely this was just a fluke (Mom was cystic). I pushed off the inevitable doctor's appointment, focusing instead on work and school. It was a particularly hectic semester, with classes in healthcare policy and ethics, grant writing, and US health systems, and my goal was to graduate sometime the following year; I didn't have the time or energy to worry about theoretical tumors. I convinced myself to hold off on scheduling a doctor's appointment until winter break.

The holiday season was busy as well, as Massimo and I were traveling to Puerto Rico for my 40th birthday celebration; I was looking forward to a beautiful pork meal. As with all our travels, my husband and I made the most of our time away from home, meeting locals, sampling delicacies, basking in the sunshine – all while I was ignoring the cloud of anxiety hanging over the festivities. When I returned to the States, I finally scheduled an appointment with my doctor, only to learn that my OBGYN wasn't in.

"That's fine, I can wait until February for my first mammogram," I assured the doctor over the phone, still hoping to ignore the problem away.

"What's the reason for the call?"

"I think I feel something."

Naturally, I was told to schedule an appointment immediately. Within hours, my life was a whirlwind of biopsies, ultrasounds, and zooming from one doctor's office to another. I was only 40 years old when I had my first and last mammogram, and I rang in the new year with undeniable news: I had breast cancer.

Of all my diagnoses, this one elicited the most contradictory reactions. Half of me was prepared to annihilate cancer, to dive into treatment with spirits high and heart strong. The other half, however, was weary from that indescribable, sinking feeling of impending mortality. I'd gotten lucky so many times before; fate had to fight back at some point, and I was terrified that this was my time.

Massimo refused to let me begin this journey with my hopes so low. As devastated as I imagine he was, he was determined to be my rock from beginning to end. Immediately after receiving my diagnosis, my husband whisked me away for a weekend in Las Vegas: Sin City! We were not going to go down without a fight. This was to be our last adventure before the reality of cancer treatments could truly set in.

There's a haunting photo of me taken right before we left for Vegas. I'm near our front window, my face turned away from the sunlight, and the long, thick hair of which I had always been so proud streaming down my back – but it's what's in the background that's important. I'm seated before a painting from my Aunt Marie's house. I always considered myself a Pagliacci and believed that the show must go on. But this time, it was different: I doubted everything in my life. Looking at that photograph, the connection between me and the frowning, painted face is almost laughably on-the-nose. After years of standing behind a fortress of smiles and positivity, my diagnosis seemed to have battered those walls, leaving me vulnerable and afraid.

I forced myself to enjoy that Vegas trip. My heart was broken and no amount of gambling, shows, food, or majestic travels in little Paris, little Venice, or little New York would change that. Massimo and I gorged ourselves on extravagant meals, walked through as many hotel lobbies as possible, and danced the nights away. I was bitterly aware of the irony surrounding me. Vegas is the epitome of life, with lights and sparkle and shine; meanwhile, I feared that death was lingering inside of me, waiting until we got home to strike. It was horrifying.

I was lucky to have the support of not only my husband and family throughout my treatment, but of my academic program as well. My bachelor's program was not as forgiving towards my missed classes and health needs; I even had to fight to get a handicapped pass after my back surgery, which rendered walking even small distances painful. Cambridge, on the other hand, accommodated all of my needs; I even had a support group at work, where I was now a secretary for the medical director and surrounded by encouragement, which I needed more than ever. I knew that this particular illness would be a marathon, not a race, so I needed to battle every obstacle with all of my willpower – but finding that inner strength would prove more difficult than I ever envisioned.

Even before I started treatment, I relearned one of the most important lessons I'd gained from my experience with radiation: there is always someone worse off than yourself. Before I lost my hair, I participated in a makeup class for women with cancer. Rather than boost my spirits as intended, the afternoon forced me to reflect on my own life. Another woman in the class was getting radiation to remove tumors in her brain; the effects were such that earlier that week, while trying to drive home, she circled the block 20 times, unable to remember what her house looked like. And here I was, feeling sorry for myself because I would be losing my hair. Really?

I knew that there was no point holding onto vanity as I entered treatment, but the reality of going bald was too difficult to ignore, so when I learned about a company in Florida that makes halo wigs with patients' own hair, I signed up immediately. I went to a wig shop, where my hair was cut following a careful set of instructions; then they shipped my beloved locks hundreds of miles south. I wore my halo – a hat with my old hair attached – whenever Massimo and I left the house.

But no matter how many makeup classes I took or wigs I made, nothing could have prepared me for how all-encompassing cancer would be. Between the weight gain, hair loss, exhaustion, and stress, glancing at a mirror felt like I was looking back into a stranger's eyes.

On top of radiation and chemotherapy, I opted for a double-mastectomy, so by the end of my cancer treatment, I was utterly transformed, inside and out. I see much of myself echoed in the works and words of Frida Kahlo, particularly in the way she embraced her pain and intimacy with mortality. I admire how she used brushes and paint to depict her physical turmoil, how she found beauty in ugliness. By the end of my cancer treatment, I hardly recognized myself, but like Frida after her near-fatal accident, I constantly aspire to accept and even love my new body. I have also lived the truth of something Frida once attested: "At the end of the day, we can endure much more than we think we can."

In the moment, cancer broke my spirit. I felt raw and vulnerable and embarrassed. In many ways, however, breast cancer was a cleansing. I learned to distinguish my spirit and mind from my outward appearance, ultimately forgoing vanity as my body transformed. And I was forced to finally care for my body and soul, to put myself first, both during treatment and during the long road to recovery.

I can pinpoint the exact moment I realized that I needed to truly listen to my body. It was during a chemo injection. "Tell us if you feel any discomfort," my doctor told me before listing off countless ways I might notice the treatment was going awry. I was confident I would be fine: I had always been a strong patient, never one to complain about something as silly as a little discomfort. Then it began: the feeling like water was filling my lungs, like I was drowning in air.

"I can't breathe," I managed to say.

Luckily, it was an easy fix – but I didn't easily shake that horrifying feeling of being trapped underwater. If I hadn't paid attention to my body and spoken up when things felt wrong, that simple injection could have turned into something much more serious.

When I started treatment, I was given a list of "Complementary and Integrative Therapies" to help me through the process. It includes dozens of treatments, some of which I had already tried and some of which were surprising: caffeine, flaxseed, focusing, guided imagery, hypnosis, meditation, mistletoe, music therapy, pet therapy, prayer, St. John's wort, Tai Chi, yoga, and zinc – to name just a handful.

The sheer array and variety of therapies is astounding. It's a reminder that every body and mind is different and requires different types of care, and that pain and hardships are never the end of the road; there are always options, even if it feels like you've exhausted them all.

And so I learned to listen to my body's messages, to let go of vanity, and to push through the chemo. With each treatment, I could feel the tumor inside of me deflating like a skewered balloon. As the chemo killed virtually everything else inside of my body, I took strength knowing that it was also killing what was making me sick. Even my mastectomy ultimately empowered me: I had no children to breastfeed, after all, and I had the once-in-a-lifetime opportunity to custom design a new pair of breasts – I even got a tummy tuck as a bonus. I took joy from the small moments throughout my cancer treatment, and as the months wore on and my body changed, I could feel that fateful day when I would be declared cancer-free draw closer.

That day came on August 5, 2015. I consider this date my second birthday: after six months of chemo and exhaustion and pain and discomfort, I had transformed into a new me. After more than 40 years of convincing myself that I was fine, even when my body was screaming at me that it was otherwise, I was finally putting myself at the forefront of my own life.

Two years later than I had hoped, I graduated with my master's degree. Despite my hiatus from school, despite years of being told my disability rendered me incapable of holding a real job, despite not having any family who had been down the path of academia to direct me – despite a lifetime of obstacles, I succeeded. Naturally, my family celebrated in typical Belli style: big, loud, and with lots of food – I even had a designer cake with my company logo on it. Soon after graduating, I opened my own consulting company to keep my body in the game.

Learning to Heal

Of course, my story isn't over – far from it. I'm three years old in cancer birthdays as of August 5, 2018, but I'm still on the long road to recovery. The effects of chemotherapy linger longer than one would expect: some days I'm so exhausted that I still feel like I'm in treatment, and other days I feel so full of life that I want to do it all.

Although my body suffers from its share of aches and pains, I now recognize when it needs a little extra love. When I feel tired, I rest; when I'm hungry, I eat; when something feels wrong, I tell a doctor. I automatically accuse myself of being selfish from time to time (old habits die hard), but I push myself to care for my body – even when it feels like my body doesn't care for me in return.

This mindset applies to mental health as well. I'm lucky to have worked in a mental health clinic and gotten a first-hand professional perspective on how mental health treatment really works. I learned how to pay attention to my mind as well as my body, so that if I sensed something significantly off, I could tell my doctor. When I started taking antidepressants, I stayed on the alert in case my prescription was the wrong fit. And I made sure to balance that psychiatric treatment with as many positive lifestyle changes as possible. I often think back to that list of alternative therapies that I received during cancer, and take comfort in knowing that even what feels like the most hopeless of days, there is some kind of remedy

I haven't tried – even if it's as simple as petting my dog or calling a loved one on the phone.

Self-care isn't easy, especially given that it's a muscle I've refused to flex most of my life. I like to compare the concept of self-care to being on an airplane, when the flight attendant informs you that you have to put on your own mask before you can help others. After all, how can you be an advocate for people in need when you can't breathe yourself? Of course, implementing this advice is easier than saying it aloud – but in the end, taking the time and energy to heal is well worth the extra effort.

This journey of mindfulness and recovery has required some major lifestyle changes. I stopped eating meat a while ago, and although I'm slowly reintroducing that extra bit of needed protein into my diet, I shop as consciously as possible, only bringing home farm-fed options. The room that Massimo and I once planned as a nursery is now my yoga studio, and I've come to terms with the fact that children may not be in our future. I do take comfort knowing that my ovary is still sitting in a freezer at Cornell, just in case, and Massimo and I are the proud parents of our tiny, darling dog Lucy. Most challenging of my self-care goals has been limiting my sugar intake. At a certain point, I just had to admit to myself that I have an unconquerable sweet tooth, so I've stuck to only eating raw sugar and trying to avoid eating cookies for breakfast – as often as possible, anyway.

My sisters and I even went on a wellness retreat together to practice self-healing. Among cancer's myriad of surprising blessings, chief among them was how it brought my sisters together after many years of bickering. For a full week, the three of us shut off our phones and engaged in intentional self-reflection. The retreat offered reiki, meditation, yoga classes, and a positive, healing energy.

Top on my list of post-cancer goals is getting back in shape. Other than a brief stint running the front desk for a fitness center after high school, I've barely set foot in a gym since I was 18. But here I am, day after day, cancer-free and lifting weights. I'm blessed to have found a fitness center that's run by a former physical therapist. I don't have to go out of my way to find accommodations, and I feel right at ease asking for help from my trainers, who challenge my body in ways I never imagined. And despite how much I strain and sweat and complain, I feel stronger every day.

After a recent workout, I got that pre-diagnosis lump in my throat again: I felt something in my arm, something bulging, something that definitely hadn't been there before. The new listen-to-your-body me rushed to my doctor's office, terrified that I'd found a tumor.

"That's a muscle!" I was told. Phew.

I was equal parts embarrassed and ecstatic. Me, building muscle! Who could have imagined that tiny, fragile girl who once came so close to death would go on to develop visible, tumor-mistakable muscles!

Of course, my newfound optimism and self-love can be difficult to maintain, especially when hardships come along. Many of my loved ones have left us – Uncle Jimmy and Nonno, Massimo's parents, as well as some of our dearest friends. Aunt Marie's passing was particularly difficult. She even stayed in our home while we were trying to determine what was wrong with her. A sudden change in personality made me suspicious – she went so far as to compliment me on my poached eggs – and she was eventually diagnosed with a brain tumor, glioblastoma. The disease was as much a blessing as it was a curse, in that she didn't feel any pain – but losing her left a gaping hole in our family.

And ever since Massimo's mother and father left us, his drive to get up and go is stronger than ever. Life, both of us have learned, is too short to spend cooped up at home. My husband even treated me and my parents to a New York extravaganza last year, complete with VIP seats to see the Rockettes and a stunning meal at a 3-star Michelin restaurant. No matter how sick or despondent I am, my husband makes sure we keep living to the fullest.

We've traveled virtually everywhere: an island cruise that took us from Granada to Aruba to Saint Thomas to Venezuela; Miami and Key West, where I fell in love with key lime pie and drag shows; the Montreal Jazz Festival; snowy Vermont; Mexico, where we have a timeshare that we adore, many times over; along the East Coast, we've been to Port Jefferson, Newport, and Martha's Vineyard, to name just a few staycation spots. And my personal adventures are never-ending: I've parasailed over the Sea of Cortez where it meets the Pacific Ocean; snorkeled with stingrays; had a fish pedicure; been to the Grotta Azzurra, or Blue Grotto, on the coast of the island of Capri; met Nikki Sixx from Motley Crue, the glamorous Heather Locklear, even Al Gore; gone sailing and learned to canoe one-handed; tasted Dom Perignon and eaten raw oysters; and shared countless meals with friends and family.

Along with my travels and self-care, I've also allowed myself to become more visible and vocal since I've entered remission. Gone are my high school days of wanting to blend into the shadows and be silent. Now, when I need something, I ask for it, whether it's a tool to make one of the exercise machines at the fitness center easier or a break from my volunteer responsibilities.

I'm also less afraid of the spotlight. When staff from my gym asked if they could feature me in a promotional video about their programs, I initially hesitated: a few short years ago, had you asked me if I wanted a video of me posted for the world to see – especially a video of me working out with my prosthesis in full view – I would have balked at the very idea. After some thought, however, I considered how this opportunity would be valuable for others, even if it made me feel awkward in the moment. If the video of me, a one-armed woman, conquering a rowing machine can inspire even one person to improve their body and life, my embarrassment would be completely worthwhile.

Bits and pieces of me have gone missing over the years – an arm, an ovary, both breasts – and I often joke that it's a wonder I'm not an addict. I've encountered more physical pain than many people encounter over a lifetime, and I understand the desire to numb oneself. Had I given in to the temptation to take my pain away, however, I wouldn't be here today; even my habit of ignoring pain has gotten me into trouble.

I'm telling my story for the same reason that I agreed to make that video for my gym: if my journey, however rocky and even embarrassing it may seem, can show someone in pain that it's worth it to persevere, then my own struggles will have been worthwhile.

For that person in pain who is reading my story, hoping to glean some miraculous words of wisdom, I wish I could offer something so simple. The truth is, I struggle every morning to make my way out of bed, to get to the gym and better myself. I try to find joy in simple moments and appreciate the people who have made my survival possible, but I recognize that gratitude is no simple task; self-pity and self-loathing are much easier mindsets to fall back on in times of strife. Along each step of my journey, no matter how impossible it seemed, I clung to the hope that my perseverance would be worth it. Radiation, chemotherapy, an amputation, a double-mastectomy, and physical therapy, not to mention countless surgeries and biopsies and diagnoses – none of these were pleasant at the time. But the joy of seeing my husband's face, of returning to work and helping people, of tasting my mother's cooking

– those moments made even the most painful of recoveries worthwhile. For anyone suffering through addiction, I can leave you with this: remember to breathe, move, and look forward. You have the power to succeed within you, even if you can't believe it right now.

It's impossible to boil my emotional and physical journey down to a simple cliché or story, but I see myself sharply reflected in the overtold tale of the donkey and the well. In case you haven't heard the story, it's about a donkey who finds himself stuck in the bottom of a deep, inescapable well. As the donkey laments his inevitable mortality, clod upon clod of dirt is heaped upon his head from above. Instead of burying himself beneath the dirt and surrendering to death, the donkey does something miraculous: with each shovel of dirt, he shakes himself off and steps up onto the fresh mound of soil, slowly lifting himself to the surface. It's a cheesy story, but profound, and for me, relatable. Many times over, I could have let myself drown beneath the pain striking my body, but I forced myself to shake it off and climb. Admittedly, the story is an over-simplification: in the real world, there is no final landing, no single moment that marks one's final release from pain. For me, however, there have been many small victories that make the mounds of dirt worthwhile: my wedding day, graduating from college, hearing the news that I was officially cancer-free, enjoying beautiful meal after beautiful meal with my family. Unlike the donkey's, my well isn't permanently full, but I have learned how to shake off the dust and grow stronger with each and every obstacle.

Recently, my husband and I went to Benevento, Italy for a family wedding, but my husband took me to Venice for some much-needed alone time. On our private excursion, he reminded of our pre-cancer Vegas adventure and how I'd refused to ride the gondola. "That was on purpose," I told him. I knew in my heart of hearts that I would make it through treatment and make it to Venice in person – and we did it, together. Massimo, you are my personal caretaker, my best friend, my husband, and my soulmate; you have been with me every step of the way. I love you, amore. Thank you.

Last year, as part of my cancer-free cleansing journey, I made one of the most foolish and brilliant decisions of my life: I decided to walk across burning hot coals. The symbolism needs little explanation: I was leaving behind my past and becoming reborn as I entered a bright future. The most terrifying part of the experience wasn't the fiery coals themselves but simply waiting in line: my heart became more frenzied with each anticipatory step forward. But somehow, I talked myself out of running away.

The coals were exactly what you would expect: prickly, coarse, and searing hot. What was surprising, however, was what my mind focused on during those brief, sizzling seconds. Instead of thinking about the flames beneath my feet or the blisters that I would have to nurse when I got back to my room, my eyes locked on what was on the other side of my path: a water hose and a blanket of cool, green grass. "Stay cool, stay cool, stay cool," I told my feet as they dashed across the coals as if with minds of their own. I was terrified, but I continued doing three things: breathing, moving, and looking forward.

I have walked through flames. I have enjoyed the cool sensation of relief on the other side. And I am never turning back.

Mom's family reunion with so many loved ones.

Mom, Dad, and Mas in Mexico.

My love in Venice – thank you!

Aunt Marie, Aunt Patty, Uncle Ralph, and Mommy – I am so blessed!

Sailboat – how fun!

Getting cozy in Cabo with my niece, Gab, and my sister, Carla.

Happy Birthday in heaven, Grandma.

Master's Graduation Party

Zia Delores, you are like a second mom to us. Thank you for being in our lives and for stepping up when we were in need. We love you!